Trees, the guardians of the soul

Mom – the ink in my pen and the power behind my words

To Denise – always supportive. Without her this book would not be written.

Published by Graysonian Press

www.graysonian.com pat@graysonian.com 0450260348

Copyright © 2009 Pat Grayson

All rights reserved under international copyright conventions. No part of this book may be reproduced, stored in a retrieval system, or transmitted in any form or by any means electronic, mechanical, photocopying, recorded or otherwise without written permission from Graysonian Press.

Printed in Australia in 2012
First printed in South Africa

Whilst every care has been taken to check the accuracy of the information in this book, the publisher cannot be held responsible for any errors, omissions or originality.

ISBN: 978-0-620-43938-1

Cover design: Tom Morrison of Ink Pot designs tim@theinkpot.net

Testimonials

"We, like Dante sometimes find ourselves lost in a dark wood with the road lost and gone. This book points to the tracks that will lead us back to the edge of the forest, back into sunlight."
Dorian Haarhoff (poet, writer and writing mentor, who is steeped in story. A former Professor of English at UCT)

In this delightful book of short stories, Pat Grayson interweaves his own eclectic mix of philosophy, hope, humour and encouragement in a way that is delightful to read and will leave you turning the page for the next story. Treat yourself to one story every day and savour the gentle message within it.
Caroline Chaplin, editor Renaissance Magazine

INTRODUCTION

When I write, there is a quantum leap from what I know to what I put down. I love where it comes from, and subsequently I have learnt much from what I have written.

My writings emerge from topics that I grapple to understand. For reference material, I use life and reverence. To read the work is to know the writer.

Each story has a message to offer, a truth - well, the way I see truth.

To get the most from these stories, only read one or two a day. If you read too many, the stories will get lost in each other. They have been categorised to make them easier to work through.

Finally, I hope you enjoy reading them as much as I enjoyed writing them.

CONTENTS

POSITIVE THINKING 1
- What Would You Do if You Knew you could not fail?. 2
- Being Dyslexic 5
- Express Yourself 9
- Collective Consciousness 10
- Life - does it have to be fair? 13
- Your roar is within you! 15

FAIRY TALES 19
- Trees - The Guardians of the Soul 21
- (an old Graysonian fairy-tale) 21
- Metamorphosis 24
- Snail Trail 29
- (another Graysonian Fairy Tale) 29
- Nature is the doorway 32

NATURE, ANIMALS AND EARTH 40
- Mother Earth 42
- Nature 43
- The Love of a Pet 45
- Life lessons 49
- Elephant Walk 51
- The Yippee Story 55

BITS AND PIECES 58
- Africa 59
- Who am I 61
- A Tribute 63
- Box Processor 66
- Dweller in the Innermost 67
- It's All Perfect 68
- My Brother John (a true story) 70
- Palms - A Natural Biography 72
- Southern Cross 73

The Initiation 79
Understanding Experience 79
The Solution 84
Turning the Tables 87
Where Has Your Energy Gone? 89
Divorce 92

SELFHELP 95

How We See Ourselves 97
Does Your Life Work? 98
Journey of Self 100
Money Mirror 102
Painting Your Life 104
Energy Is the Thought 105
The Creator Within 106
In Action There Is Hope 108
Self-worth 110
Time and People -Exhaustible 114
and Precious 114
In Days of Old 115
The Pain of Glass 118
Awareness 120
Mind Evaluator 122

SPIRITUAL 126

Impermanence 127
Oneness 129
Creating God in Our Image 132
Angel Wings 133
Robbed at Gunpoint 134
Christ – the Extraordinary 136
Bodyverse (Part One) 139
Bodyverse (Part Two) 143
Bodyverse (Part Three) 146
In the Name of God 148

Help from the Other Side 152
Is Death a Rebirth? 153
Bully Beef, Dried Biscuits the Folly of War 155
Can I Bring My BMW with Me? 161
That is what Oneness is made of 164

POSITIVE THINKING

What Would You Do if You Knew You Could not Fail?

The applause was deafening as he ambled to the podium. Although stooped, he carried an air of confidence and distinction that age could not disguise. Somehow he seemed larger than his diminutive self. Shaggy white hair flopped over his wide forehead. Enormous eyebrows sheltered bright sparkling eyes, eyes that twinkled with intelligence. His clothes were those of a gentleman who walks in the park. Not dapper nor pretentious; comfortable perhaps? Most notable was his smile, wide and authentic, the smile of a man who has had a satisfying life.

Finally reaching the podium, he leaned on it for support. As the attendant helped with placing the mike on Dr Jennings's lapel, he surveyed the audience. He did this with confidence and interest. He saw eager young faces, the faces of the graduates to whom the day belonged. They were the cream of the MBA students who were to be capped after his speech.

His first words were hardly audible, almost as if they were to himself. The students leaned forward, straining to hear. They did not want to miss a word from this captain of industry, whose modest beginnings had not prevented him from becoming a household name. With more focus and louder this time, he said, 'What would you do if you knew you could not fail?' Still, it was offered as if his mind were elsewhere and, as the students followed his speech, they learned that it was.

He was reminiscing about a time, sixty-eight years earlier, when he was fourteen. He talked about a dream he had had. A profound dream, that had directed the course of his life, shaped him as an icon, not only in his own country but around the world. In the dream, he saw himself determinedly striding up a mountain, higher and higher, short of breath, tired, but driven. Onwards he continued, passing gnarled, stunted trees and ice-covered moss until, in mist and cold, he reached the summit. Immediately, he heard a friendly voice, 'So you finally made it?'

Positive Thinking

Peering into the swirling haze, he saw an elfin man, with a long white beard and bushy hair that seemed to merge with the fog. 'Sit down on this stone and rest, for I have a message that I am to pass on to you.'

Some forty-five minutes later, zombie-like, he made his way back down the mountain, with the words of the elfin man ringing in his ears, '"Live your life as if you cannot fail." 'And so, ladies and gentleman, I did,' announced Dr Jennings. 'I had the mantra *I cannot fail* guiding me all these years. Consequently, I did not have the insecurities that seem to inhibit most of society. I recommend that you contemplate what you would do if you knew you could not fail.'

He became quiet, letting that last thought sink in. 'You would be dauntless, navigating through life's impediments, as if they did not exist. Knowing that you could not fail would give you the confidence to embark on any project, in any situation, knowing that you would win. With no thought of ridicule, your creativity would flow. With the outcome assured, you would work with zeal for the early fruition of all that you did. You would do more in your life and there would no procrastination. Imagine the tasks you could accomplish in your allotted time, if you knew that there was no risk!'

Other than his voice, there was not a sound; all eyes were trained on Dr Jennings, totally intent on imbibing the wisdom that was offered to them.

'By knowing that you could not fail, and because of your positive, no-nonsense approach, you would attract a willing band of supporters, all carried along by your vision and unconquerable will. When you have thoughts of failure, there are barriers. When you believe in yourself, there can be no obstacles, or none that are insurmountable. You would not be paralysed as most of humanity is when confronted with a dilemma. With the mantra, *I cannot fail*, you would always find solutions. Because you would experience no scarcity, you would have no greed. What you built would be for the good of all.'

He then paused, to let the magnitude of what he was saying sink in. He resumed, 'When you know that you cannot fail, you will not have self-esteem issues. There would be no space for them in your consciousness. Knowing that you cannot fail permits you to live without the necessity for a large ego.' Then lowering his voice for emphasis, he added, 'Life is so much simpler when there is no need for airs or graces, or to impress.'

He continued along these lines for some time, with the students clinging to every utterance. Then, by way of winding-up, with his assured smile, he said, 'The premium is probably in the relationships you will form. I have been married for fifty-two years. They have been good years, very good years, and do you know why? I married because I knew I could not fail! I was not afraid to be myself - there was no pretence. Knowing that I could not fail granted me the freedom to allow my wife, Mary, to be who she was.'

When he finished, the ovation was long and thunderous. For a few moments he just stood there, with that open smile, knowing that once again he had not failed and that the guidance he had received from the mystic would continue to guide others.

That was thirty-six years ago. Mine was one of those eager young faces and I have never forgotten his message. He has long departed, but his legacy remains. I embraced his words "I cannot fail", and they have served me well.

Being Dyslexic

Damn it. Once again I bank 103 instead of 301 bucks. I'm dyslexic and, as you read this, you'll see that being dyslexic has governed my entire life, sometimes in amusing ways, like the time when I thought I would try my hand at Internet dating. Instead of selecting the contender's age range of 36 to 47. I flagged 36 to 74. Can you imagine my horror when a toothless, prune-faced geriatric beamed at me as I opened my e-mail?

Dyslexia is derived from two Greek words, *Dys* – meaning poor or inadequate and *Lexis* – words or language. According to research the cortex has six basic layers, with layer one having essentially no cells, but dyslexics typically have bunches of cells in layer one.

It seems that dyslexia is a disease of the fortunate, as research indicates that you have to be above average intelligence to have it. And here is the killer for you feminists -- males are three times more likely to have it than females. But then I am not too sure about the research ... such as, why would they use mice to look at encoding phonological or temporal processing?

A friend once asked me how my dyslexic brain functions. 'It works,' I told her, as if it were correct and the rest of the world wrong. It has a method of its own, like that of some sort of strange animal species that evolved in an unknown pocket of wilderness. I have no problem with maths and can add as quickly as anyone. But when I am trying to spell a word, it is as though the connections come adrift. I get stuck in a sort of limbo. This is probably the reason why I spell the same word in a document many different ways, and each looks correct to me. My mind won't be boxed in and limit the word to only one spelling.

In my first year of school I could not form the written letters of the alphabet, like prissy Mary could. I moved my tongue out of my mouth with the effort of writing, but the result was still a mess. It was as if the pencil had a will of its own. This was the start of my being labelled as being 'different'. I was held back at the end of that first year, to 'try again' with another bunch of kids.

In time I discovered that there were more and more things that I couldn't cope with. The label 'different' was later amended to 'dunce'. Yet I didn't feel stupid. But as time went on I told myself, 'Maybe this is what being stupid is like.'

The school system, and the ability to form neat *r*'s or *j*'s, was the measure. School is still the standard by which our intellectual capacity or lack of it is gauged. It didn't take long before I lost faith in school, thought of myself as hopeless and blocked learning even more. I developed a brittle self-esteem and became an unfulfilled and angry person.

If there was one area in my life that helped to salvage some self-respect it was on the sports field, as I fared better than most. Without the balance of sport, I would indeed have been in a sorry state.

A new school year was always interesting as the incoming teacher either unconsciously or consciously classified the children. It was never long before I was relegated to the back of the class, considered a waste of time. Provided I behaved I was generally ignored. That was forty odd years ago. Schools may be different today.

Of course, I wasn't quiet and well behaved and through expressing myself I disrupted the class. So not only did the teacher consider me 'slow', but a nuisance as well.

Year after sorry year passed with me sliding further back into academic oblivion. I became angrier and more rebellious. Year three of high school saw 'them' putting pressure on me to leave. This was just fine by me and, as ironic as it may seem, I left school to get an education.

Only later, when Mom saw the same elements in my young brother, did she set out to find an answer. Her studies culminated in her becoming a remedial teacher. By that time I had left home. Visiting one night, she explained about dyslexia. I'd never heard of the word and thought, 'so what?'. She wanted to train me with remedial techniques but, being touchy about the matter, I made all sorts of excuses. I was fine as a bricklayer and occasional drunk.

Positive Thinking

Fortunately, as the years passed, I gained confidence in myself as a person. The inadequacies receded and became less important. My child-like writing, atrocious spelling and the mixing of numbers did not concern me any more.

The brain is a wonderful organism and over the years mine has, to a degree, trained itself to reverse errors. For instance, I might be looking for 93 and upon seeing the number say 'ah, there's 39', but I know it is 93 as an instantaneous reversal would have taken place.

In my work I conduct presentations to executives with lots of notes on flip charts. Seldom is there a time when a dyslexic slip-up doesn't make an appearance. An example could be where I start to write the word *bank*, but it appears on the board as *bnak*. There are other times when *bank* appears as *nbka*. In other words, I would write first the *b* and then the *n*, which I'll squeeze in to the left of the *b,* and so on.

When I produce any of these unintended gems I'm not aware of the awkward sequence. In my mind it is normal spelling. The adjustments are made without conscious thought. In fact, I may only realise something abnormal has happened if I notice the audience casting flabbergasted looks towards the board as if to say, 'Whoa, did you see that?'

I'm often amused at the universe's sense of humour when it conjured me up as a dyslexic person while laying a path to make me a writer. Or is it rather the intelligence of the universe? And what about timing? I couldn't have managed in commerce if I'd been born twenty years earlier. My hand-written correspondence wouldn't have been of an acceptable standard. The corporates would have disposed of me, like a pack of wild dogs abandoning an injured or aged member. I was given the handicap and, at the same time, a personal computer with a phenomenal spell-check!

On the subject of machines, an ATM can provide a fascinating experience for me. I usually have no problem getting my pin number out of my head. But if, at the time, someone near me mentions another number, for instance a telephone number, then my mind becomes jumbled and I can't get the pin number into the ATM correctly. I remember watching helplessly as one card was consumed, never to be seen again, by an overzealous machine, as

Positive Thinking

a result of my confusing the number. When I get the jumbles, it's best for me to leave the ATM, reformat the hard disk of my brain and return later.

Continuing with the answer to my friend, I told her that my mind has difficulty deciphering gothic or fancy script. Most cursive writing is gobbledygook and has to be read to me. But I also told her that being dyslexic has forced me to become the achiever that I am today. If I am in front of a group of executives, I don't care about my scrawl. I have learned to establish my own worth, and not to allow society to provide the rules by which my value is measured. Empowered, I have risen from an almost illiterate bricklayer at twenty-two, to owning and managing my own international computer software company, where I design software for business use.

It is late, 25:12 a.m., and time for bed.

Express Yourself

Compare your life to that of a tree
At first a seed -- you a foetus
The seed germinates; you are born
Strong green shoots search for sunlight
You reach for your mother's breast and experiences
The sapling gets stronger, firmly burying roots in nurturing soil;
while you walk, speak and start to express individuality
Years pass, the tree has grown and although not yet full height,
does not blow or wash away
You have grown to fend for yourself; life is spread before you

STOP!

What happens next?
The tree can remain in shadow, scrambling for sunlight
It has a choice -- remain stunted or express itself
You have the same choice--grow or remain unfulfilled
It is in the tree's genes to shrug off inadequacy; to grow strong, tall and ever upwards,
arcing towards the sky and taking its place in the sun
What about you, can you claim your natural right and shrug off imperfection,
or do you languish in the shade of others, stunted and withered?

Collective Consciousness

I was impatient for Father to arrive as this was my favourite time of the week. It was our time together, without interruptions. For two hours he would teach me wisdom that would normally be beyond my years. Our time together was a time when he was relaxed and laughed and was able to cherish the moment.

When he arrived, his joy and enthusiasm gave him a childlike look. His advisors discreetly remained and closed the door behind him. He embraced me with an affectionate hug.

After the preliminaries, when he had asked about my studies of the past week, we settled down on the floor. I watched his handsome and intelligent face as he started off by saying, 'You are aware that the planet Earth lags far behind us, yet there was a time when Earthlings and Polsorites were of equal accomplishments?'

This was given as both a statement and a question. I nodded and he continued, 'Polsorite and Earth came out of the same big bang and as a result have much in common. For instance, both have oxygen, water and plants growing on their surfaces. Earthlings look different from us but have an organ that is similar to ours and that is the brain. What separates us from them is that we direct our brain, whereas earthlings allow the brain to run riot and think what it wants to think.'

Father paused here to let me absorb what he had said and then went on. 'Where we quickly learnt that thoughts manifest what they are focused on, earthlings never made the connection. We are taught from birth that negativity destroys and that positivity builds. This is on both an individual and a collective basis. The collective thought of all Polsrites govern the state, our planet. It is the collective positive thought that makes Polsrite so healthy and abundant.'

He shook his head in a sad way and said, 'But humans got into the habit of having predominately negative thoughts, and look at the results -- a seething morass of poison, damaged ozone, places of war, pestilence and famine. They have all but destroyed the Earth.'

I interrupted him to ask, 'Father, are the people of Earth aware of us?'

'No, they are not. In fact, we have tried to help them many times but to no avail. For instance, we sowed into their philosophy the dictum of *Love thy neighbour*, but sadly they do the opposite, and anyone who seems different from themselves is perceived to be a threat. Even now, as we talk, there are wars raging in many parts of Earth where thousands are dying. And so, not only are the lives of individuals on Earth curtailed by the negativity, but their planet is also clogged by unhealthy energy.

'We are blessed here on Polsrite as we have happiness, love, health and abundance. And because we chose to be positive, we developed the same vibration as the creative aspect of the Source and therefore evolved very quickly.

'Earthlings on the whole have never made that link, and so they remain primitive and self-destructive; stuck with a "pre-cultured" mindset. On earth they are actually taught things like mathematics and the sciences - not like us, who in our advanced stage of mind-use are able to simply absorb this knowledge by tapping into the Universal Source. Some Earthlings study until midlife to learn only what we are able instantly to know.'

All of this made me consider just how backward man must be and I felt sorry for them. If only they could learn to think positively!

Father continued, 'They understand that the brain is a device which can be filled with knowledge but their focus is on things, where our "thought-school" focuses on connecting with the Super Conscious. Even now, only a few Earthlings understand that each individual is the sum total of their thinking. They certainly don't understand the power of collective thought and that Earth is dying because of the negative sum total of all men's thoughts since mankind began to think. Unless they learn to control fear, greed, xenophobia, moral decay and the like, their planet will perish as will all humans, plants and animals on it.'

As he paused, I asked, 'You said, on the whole they have never made the connection. Does that imply that some are enlightened?'

His face beamed, 'Oh, my boy, you follow the learning with intelligence,' while he gave me a quick affectionate rub on my back. 'Yes, there have been some who through self-discipline reached a state of awareness. One was called Jesus Christ and another was known as the Buddha. In fact, there have been many, and most became teachers. But mankind is too limited to live the teaching. They are too greedy, angry and resentful and all of those other concepts you have been fortunate enough never to have had experienced.

'At the moment, there is a small groundswell of people who have worked to gain clarity. We support these few brave individuals in the swaying of the minds of the masses. It could all change if each individual were to claim the personal power that is inscribed into his genetic make-up. They must shed the meekness that incapacitates them *as mass awareness happens on an individual basis.*'

It was all too soon when a soft knock told us that our time was already up. Father smiled as if to say matters of state are calling.

When he was gone, I slowed my mind down and tapped into the Creative Source to get a glimpse of man on Earth. After only a few seconds I backed out as the energy there was too dismal. As I cleared the heaviness from my mind I pondered on something Father had said -- that mass awareness happens on an individual basis.

I then expressed the creed that Polsrites recite in early lessons, and sent it to earth with all the love that I could muster.

> When there is trust in the heart, there is love in the person.
> If there is love in the person, there will be harmony in the home.
> If there is harmony in the home, there will be harmony on the street.
> If there is harmony on the street, there will be harmony in the suburb, the city and the planet.
> If there is harmony on the planet, there will be peace.
> When there is peace, there is love.

I then shouted, 'Good luck, Earth, you can do it!'

Positive Thinking

Life - does it have to be fair?

The wild dog cautiously led her five cubs away. Having been out of the den for only two weeks, they were small and clumsy, but instinct had warned her of danger.

The young male lion had been prowling for three days and was hungry. He had been chased away from his pack, as it was time to fend for himself and create his own pride in another territory.

Coming over a rise, a movement caught his eyes. Crouching, he scanned the lush, green bush. There he spied a pack of wild dogs, the male in the lead. The mother was constantly shepherding her young, who were full of play and excitement, thinking that the outing was a game. After a few short-tempered nips on the ear, they sensed her seriousness.

The lion had been well trained by his mother and was patient. If he rushed he could lose the prey. Nor did he let out his fearsome roar, as this would have warned the dogs.

Watching them with close attention, he considered his strategy; going for the young would force the adults to attack him. However, if he ambushed the lead dog, the female would run with her cubs and leave him to fend for himself as best as he could. Yes, that would be the way.

Slinking with stealth and tracking a parallel course, he wanted to meet the dog on open ground. He was not concerned about detection as there was no breeze and plenty of cover. Further along was the open ground that he sought and increased his speed to get there at the same time as his prey.

As hunter and hunted broke cover, the lion accelerated into a loping run. Thick armour-like shoulders powered the body forward, while his perfectly still head held total focus on the lead dog. With tail lowered and ears erect, he was beautiful, but devastating.

Simultaneously the dog saw the lion and feared that he was in trouble. Instinct and reflexes came to the fore in an attempt at survival. Somewhere in his mind he knew that he had to direct the lion away from the pups, but it was already too late.

What Would You Do if You Knew You Could Not Fail?

Positive Thinking

The lion, with speed and power, leaped onto the terrified dog, its huge claws digging into his hide, while his weight pinned the dog to the ground.

At this point, it is possible that the dog's brain-chemical would have changed and it is unlikely that he would have felt the lion biting his windpipe, suffocating him. Death came swiftly.

We cannot judge the lion by our rules, but must understand that many things in life do not seem fair. This meal was not just for the lion, it was for many other creatures – jackals and vultures, ants and other microscopic animals. Nothing is wasted. Even the herbivore eats from the plant kingdom!

The female dog was aware of the death of her mate. As humans, we cannot measure an animal's grief, but it is likely that there is an acceptance of life's harshness. She, in turn, has to take the lives of other animals to feed herself and her cubs, and knows that one animal's tragedy is another's meal.

It is us humans who consider life to be unfair and let it affect us in negative ways. We retain the thought that life is tough long after an event has passed, allowing it to reduce our power.

Although life can be harsh, it can also be beautiful, provided you get on with it. When you have been bullied and brutalised, as you will be in one form or another, you must remain aware of your place in the universe. When you live in the 'life is not fair' camp you lose your balance.

You can moan, whine and feel sorry for yourself or you can put it behind you, and, like the female dog, let it go and get on with life. Winners know that life does not have to be fair in order to win, and win you can with the right attitude!

Positive Thinking

Your roar is within you!

Little Lion was only 2 years old and wanted to roar like her Daddy, Shumba. But her roar seemed not to be there and only came out as a squeak.

Worried, Little Lion said to her Daddy, 'Daddy I am so sad, I can't roar. I have tried and tried.'

Shumba was wise and said in a soft loving way, 'Your roar is inside you; you don't have to try and force it out. It will come when needed.'

Little Lion said in a rush, 'Where inside me, I can't see it, I can't feel it, what do you mean, inside of me?'

'Well, it is hard to explain,' said Shumba 'but when we are born, we are given what we need to survive. We are given muscle to fight with. We are also given speed and cunning, which allow us to catch our prey. But our roar is the power that puts it all together. Without the roar, our speed, strength and cunning would not work very well.'

Timidly, Little Lion said, 'But roar is only sound'.

'No, it is much more than that. Our roar is an expression of our strength, our will to fight, our determination. Our roar is our knowing that we are king of the jungle! But as I said, it is inside of you.'

'Oh,' is all Little Lion could say as she wandered off through the scrubby bush. *What does he mean, it is insidef me?* she wondered.

I know, I will ask Elephant. He is very smart and has such a good memory, I am sure that he will know, and so Little Lion hurried off towards the river, where the trees grow tall and strong. 'Good morning Elephant. Please may I ask you a question?'

Elephant stretched his wrinkled trunk high up to grab a branch. With slow, but determined strength, Elephant pulled the branch until there was a sharp crack. As it broke the branch fell to the ground.

What Would You Do if You Knew You Could Not Fail?

Positive Thinking

Elephant placed one big foot on the branch to hold it firm, whilst his trunk broke it into a short length that fitted comfortably into his mouth.

Little Lion was grateful that the foot that was on the branch was not on her body.

Elephant paused his graceful rhythm of reach, pull, break and eat and with small smiling eyes looked at Little Lion and said, 'How can I help?'

'Elephant, Shumba, my Daddy, said that my roar is my power and that it is inside of me, but I am afraid that I will not find it.'

Elephant said in a voice that was strong and forceful, 'If you can face your fear, as you face your reflection in the river - you will find your roar. Yes, it is within you.'

And with that, as if all that needed to be said, had been said, Elephant resumed the rhythm of reach, pull, break and eat.

Feeling just as confused, Little Lion moped along and saw Owl sitting regally in a tree. Little Lion thought, *perhaps she will know where my roar is. After all, Owl sits and sees the going's on, all night.*

As Little Lion got closer, Owl said, "Who who, goes there?"
'It's me, Little Lion,' said Little Lion.
'Owl, I have a terrible problem. I am a lion, and I am supposed to roar, but I can't. My Daddy, Shumba, said that my roar is an expression of my power, and Elephant said that if I can face my fear, as I can face my reflection in the river, then I will find my roar.'
And with that, she looked into the wise face of Owl and waited for an answer.
'So, you have not found your voice yet?'
'No I haven't.'
'Do you not know that you must change the way you think about yourself - after all, if you think of yourself only as Little Lion, that's all you will be. You must see yourself, powerful and strong, like you see Shumba - now there's a lion', said Owl with a hint of a shudder.

What Would You Do if You Knew You Could Not Fail?

Positive Thinking

And with that Owl flew off to investigate another area of her domain, but as she went she hooted, 'Remember, your roar is inside of you!'

Despondent and with her head hanging down, Little Lion continued along the path, but was startled when she heard, 'Haa, what on earth is wrong with you?' Spat Cobra, 'you could have stood on me and I would have been forced to bite you.'
'Oh, I'm sorry Cobra. I have looked for my roar everywhere and just can't find it. My Daddy, Shumba, said that my roar is an expression of my power and Elephant said that if I can face my fear, as I can face my reflection in the river, then I will find my roar. Owl said that I must see myself, not as Little Lion, but more like my powerful Daddy. But I still don't understand. In fact, I don't even know what to look for, let alone what to find.'

Cobra raised himself vertically to the same height as Little Lion's face and simply said, 'What they are all talking about is your spirit.'
'My spirit, what do you mean?'
'Your spirit is within you, waiting to be released. That is what they mean by your roar.'
'Released, huh?'
Cobra thought of himself as an intellectual and launched into what was likely to be a long explanation, 'Well, it is all a question of understanding that we animals, not just you felines, have the creative power of the Universe within us. Some would call it strength of character, whilst others refer to it as positivity. But we of the reptile kingdom refer to it as spirit. Now, if you take the left and right hemispheres of the brain ... at this stage a sad Little Lion continued her way back towards her family and home, but some thirty seconds later Little Lion could hear Cobra shout, 'Hey where are you going? Oh well, it does not matter, but remember your roar is within you!'

Oh great, everyone tells me how easy 'it' is, and that 'it', whatever it' means, is within us all and that all I have to do is to know that 'it' is there and 'it' will be released. It's easy for them.

These were the thoughts that filled Little Lion as she crested the last hill. They were quickly shooed away when she saw her younger brother, Prince, cowering. A pack of wild dogs had surrounded him,

Positive Thinking

their menace obvious. Without thinking, Little Lion charged down the hill and as she did, she let out a Roooaaar so loud that the entire valley shook - birds shrieked out of trees, whilst rocks tumbled off cliff faces. A minute later the distant hills threw back the Roooaaar. It was so loud, it sounded like thunder.

The terrified dogs ran in all directions and were far away, long before the roar finely settled and the valley returned to normal.

As they walked home, Little Lion was proud that she had saved Prince and finally understood what the wise folk of the bush had told her. She knew her roar was an expression of her power and realised, that even though she was scared of so many wild dogs, she ran towards them anyway, and so she had faced her fear, just like Elephant said.
Owl was right when she said, 'See yourself, not as a Little Lion, but powerful like Shumba,' and although Cobra drove her nuts, she also knew what he was talking about when he said 'Your spirit is inside you and you don't have to go looking, for it is already there.'

And so now Little Lion knew her roar - it was her strength, her potential and her determination, but most of all, she knew it was within her.

FAIRY TALES

Trees – The Guardians of the Soul (an old Graysonian fairy-tale)

'Do I have to go to bed, Daddy? I'm not tired.'

'Yes, my sweetie. Come on, I'll tuck you in,' said her father.

Susan was six years old and as cute as a button. Blonde hair fringed cheeky blue eyes, and a band of freckles covered her cheeks and nose like love dust.

Already clean after her bath and wearing her pyjamas, she was quick to clamber onto her bed. Busily she organised her five teddy bears around her, while dispatching the surplus pillows to the floor. She snuggled down so deeply that the duvet was up to her chin. She loved this time with her daddy and giggled with joy.

'Daddy, please say my prayers'

Sitting on the edge of her bed, her dad gently recited: 'Now I lay me down to sleep, I pray the Lord my soul to keep. If I die before I wake, I pray the Lord my soul to take. Amen.'

Susan said nothing and seemed thoughtful, until she asked, 'Daddy, where do our souls go when we sleep?'

'Gee sweetie, I don't know. Perhaps we can ask Mommy in the morning; she may know. But now you must close your eyes and wander off to sleep.' He kissed her and held her so that their cheeks touched and whispered, 'Mommy and Daddy love you very much. Sleep well, my baby.'

It was not long until she was fast asleep. In her dreams an angel appeared. Susan knew it was an angel as she had seen her before. She felt safe with her and simply called her 'Angel'. Angel had large transparent wings and a pretty face that reminded Susan of the princess in her picture book.

Angel held out her hand for Susan to take and said, 'We are going to see the guardians of the souls.' Before Susan knew it she was floating out of her body, melting through the roof and up into the night sky.

Fairy Tales

It was dark outside and the entire world seemed to be fast asleep. As she flew she felt no sensation of hot or cold, nor was there any sound. It was as if she was in a bubble. Across the city and into the hills they went and although it was night, all was clear.

They stopped moving and while floating, her angel friend said, 'Look at the trees. What do you see?'

'Those trees,' answered Susan. 'What's so special about them?'

'Look closer,' the smiling angel suggested.

Susan squinted in an effort to see better and after a time asked, 'What are those white things hanging from the trees like washing?'

Angel laughed at the description and said, 'They are souls being cleansed.'

'Cleansed?' asked Susan, very confused.

The angel said, 'Before you went to sleep, you asked where the souls went when their owners are asleep. Here they are.'

Hovering, but as comfortable as if she was sitting on her favourite lounge chair, Susan listened while Angel told her, 'When people fall into a deep sleep, their souls leave the body for energising and travel to the trees where they hang, as you said, like washing.'

'Look!' shouted Susan with glee. 'Are they fairies?' She pointed to the trees.

'Yes,' said Angel, 'they assist with the cleaning of the souls and one of their tasks is to ask the breeze to blow, which helps to purify the soul of the day's problems.'

Susan looked closer at the fairies; they were tiny, about the size of a small fly, and their wings vibrated so quickly they were just a blur. They had impish, pixie-like faces and were clothed in a variety of silky material of pastel shades. All were very busy. Some were sweeping the souls, while others were wiping and polishing.

Angel continued, 'Others also help with the cleaning. The moon sends moonbeams and the stars share their twinkle. If you look at the ground you will see gnomes cleaning up all the dirt that drops from the souls. So you see, Susan, your soul and all other souls are kept spotlessly clean by the hard work of many. When you wake up

Trees, the guardians of the soul

each morning your soul is back in place, sparkling clean and ready for a new day. If you listen, you will hear the song of the trees.'

The wind on the soul, it gets rid of the soil, tra laa laa laa.
Go to the tree to have a rest, it won't be long before you're at your best, tra laa laa laa.
Fairies and gnomes, wind and stars, trees and moon will have you ready soon, tra laa laa laa.

Susan was captivated. She could see the souls change colour from dullness to a gleaming white that sparkled like sun on a rippled stream.

The trees seemed to smile as they gently danced in the breeze. There was a sheen around them, an aura, a glow of light.

'Is my soul here?' asked Susan

'Yes it is. Look over to the Jacaranda tree.'

Susan was delighted to see a smiling and happy soul wave at her. She waved back and asked her angel, 'Why am I on that tree?'

'Well, different souls go to different trees and because yours is a happy soul it goes to a glorious and vibrant tree. Sad souls go to Weeping Willows and old souls go to Box Elders, whilst others get refreshed in Pine trees. Oh look,' pointed the angel, 'that soul is about to go home to its body.'

Susan saw a radiant fellow float from a tree, saying, 'Dear me, I must rush as my body will be waking soon.' It added, in a sing-sorg voice, 'Thank you, fairies, for all your help; bless you, gnomes, you are wonderful.' The gnomes, clearly bashful, blushed. The soul continued, 'God be with you. I'll see you all tomorrow night.' And with a whoosh the soul sped off to its body.

The angel smiled at Susan and said, 'Come, child, it is time to go.'

The next morning, Susan opened her eyes and with joy in her heart remembered her adventure of the night before. She sat up and opened the curtains to view the garden and whispered to all the trees, 'I love you - you guardians of the soul.'

Trees, the guardians of the soul

Metamorphosis

The caterpillar lay inside its cocoon and through the overlapping threads watched the world go by through a hole in the wall. He felt rotten. 'Blah, why me? Why am I stuck in this rut, and am I ever going to get out of here?'

Suddenly a beautiful creature floated towards him. For a moment the grub was transfixed and forgot his woes. As he watched, he delighted in the colourful wings, the smile on the creature's face and the way in which it joyfully floated from here to there in a dance of joy. Grub thought, 'You can afford to be happy, you're stunning and free,' but bellowed in a disgruntled way to the creature, 'Hey you, whoever you are, come here!'

The creature stopped and approached the cocoon. Peering into the hole, it said in a gentle voice, 'Why, hello. I'm a butterfly.'

Without any formality and with irritation the grub asked, 'Why are you so happy?'

The butterfly, in that same soft voice, answered, 'I'm happy because I choose to be happy and you're sad because you choose to be sad.'

'Thanks for nothing,' moaned Grub. 'It's OK for you to talk. Look at how magnificent you are, with your amazing orange wings with their black tips, while here I am stuck in this dungeon, all trussed up and unable to move. Boy, I don't even have legs, let alone wings.'

'Gee, you *are* down! You might like to know that I was once in a dark hole just like you. I remember how horrible it was.'

'So what did you do to get out of *your* hell?'

Butterfly smiled to himself as he remembered that time and then said, 'You know, Grub, it is so simple that you are unlikely to believe it.'

Grub became agitated and said, 'If it's so simple, for caterpillars' sake tell me before I go nuts!'

'Well,' the other said gently, 'If I tell you, do you promise to take the advice, no matter how simple it may seem, and try it every day for two weeks?'

'I will, I will,' said Grub urgently.

'OK, if you are willing to give it a go, the first thing is to stop struggling to get out of there – just relax.'

'How does not struggling help to get me out of here?'

Butterfly answered, 'When we force things to happen out of fear or impatience, we tend to push that which we want away. Trust me on this. Do you think you can do that?'

'Easy peezy,' said Grub.

'The second thing to do is to see yourself not as a grub in a hole but a beautiful butterfly with the breeze at your back and the sun on your wings. And can you do that as well?'

'I'll try,' he said, but with doubt in his voice.

'You'll have to do more than try; you'll have to believe it. If you don't believe, you will not become it.'

'Hmm, how can I be it, if I'm not it?' Grub pondered.

'It is, as I said, very simple. And the third thing to do is to be happy. To glow inside.'

'Now you've really lost me,' Grub said. 'You try being happy living in this grotto!'

'But you can and you have to if you want to change.' Butterfly paused, rubbing his wings together in a way that seemed very natural to Grub.

'Tell me Grub, do you think I am beautiful?'

'Oh Butter, you are magnificent. I wish I could be just like you.'

'Well, you can if you do as I say, but let me tell you that the outward beauty you see is a result of inner beauty. You know, when my time is up and I pass on, the first thing that my body loses is its colour. But now I must float off. Remember, it is up to you to change yourself. If you don't, you will just remain a caterpillar forever.'

He fluttered away, but suddenly returned and, as an afterthought, said, 'I will come in a day or two and check on your progress. Bye for now.'

This time he did go. Grub watched Butterfly float, first this way and that, in a waltz of delight and joy. Higher and further he went until he disappeared into the dark green foliage of the trees on the mountain.

Grub turned over and, staring at the black nothingness of his home, thought about what Butterfly had told him. 'Could it be so simple?' he wondered. 'Yes, it is true that I am more concerned with my worries than with happiness and I do moan a lot.' He decided to try what Butterfly suggested. For two weeks he would chase unpleasant thoughts from his mind and let it be filled only with happiness.

He started the process by marking fourteen days on his ceiling and set about being happy - seeing himself as beautiful and, as Butterfly had said, 'with a gentle breeze behind him and the sun at his back'.

It was hard but Grub was determined. As he ticked off day one, he wondered if he had changed in any way. He was not sure but felt a little happier within himself; he even laughed a bit.

On day three the light from the hole was suddenly darkened. He heard Butterfly saying softly, 'Hey, Grub. I can see you are happier and that you have a smile on your face.'

Grub returned the greeting and asked, 'How are you doing, Butter?'

After a chat, Grub watched Butterfly take off and thought to himself, 'It is nice to have a friend like Butter to help me.'

By day five, Grub woke up with an odd feeling on his back. Something was stirring. He quickly turned around to catch it, but saw nothing.

On day six, that strange feeling was even more pronounced, but he could not figure it out. When the light from the hole disappeared, he became excited as he was sure that Butter had popped over to visit. 'Is that you, Butter?'

'Yes it is. How are you doing, Grub?' When Butterfly's eyes adjusted to the light, he could see partially developed wings on

Grub's back. Chuckling to himself, he said, 'Well, well, you are really Metamorphosing.'

'What's Metamorphosing?' asked Grub.

'Just be patient and you'll see. You certainly have made great progress.'

'Do you think so?' asked a grateful Grub.

On day ten he noticed that his home was unravelling. With this he started to panic. 'What will happen if I have to leave this place? It's all I know!' He could not work it out, but was sure that it had something to do with his new way of thinking.

As if reading his thoughts, Butterfly appeared and said, 'Hey, Grub, you are almost there. In fact, I can't call you Grub any more. You are glorious.'

'What do you mean, glorious? I'm just me.'

'Well, now you are, but you weren't before.'

'Oh, so what does it all mean and what am I supposed to do now?'

'Nothing,' said Butterfly happily. 'You'll know what to do when the time comes.'

The day slid to a close with Grub feeling very happy.

It was all too soon that the cocoon disintegrated. 'Oh, oh, what now?' thought Grub, and sat there waiting for inspiration. 'There it goes again - that fluttering!' But now it was stronger than before.

Suddenly he felt himself rising. 'Help! What's happening?' he shouted. In a panic, he froze. This caused him to sink back to the ground.

When he landed, he let the fluttering start again and he rose again. It was then that he realised that he could fly, but he crashed into a tree and flopped to the ground.

'Whoa, I can fly, but now I have to learn to steer!' he thought with joy. And so off he went, happy and free.

Butterfly glided up beside him, and with quickly vibrating wings said, 'What does it feel like to be free?'

Fairy Tales

'It feels wonderful,' Grub laughed, as he scooted all over the place.

Butterfly asked, 'Have you seen what you look like?'

'No!' he replied. Butterfly suggested that he float to the pond to look at himself.

Grub did this and gently landed on a twig suspended over the water. He was scared to look at his reflection and instead took note of the glen he was in. It seemed magical; the rays of the sun searched through subdued light and water lilies in the pond exuded a tranquillity that suggested, 'It is OK - look down.'

After taking a deep breath, he lowered his gaze and took in the most beautiful sight he could imagine. 'No, it can't be me,' he thought, and to see if it was, he moved his head. As the reflection moved too, his heart quickened with excitement and joy. It was then that he noticed his wings. They were turquoise with white spots that gave him a fresh and clean look. A tear rolled down his cheek and splashed away his image - he was more beautiful than he could ever have hoped for!

And so it was that with understanding, that by being what he wanted to be, and by just letting it happen, that grub metamorphosed into his true potential, a butterfly – and so can you, if you allow it to happen.

Dedicated to Milena, a beautiful butterfly

Snail Trail
(another Graysonian Fairy Tale)

Susan put on her light blue pinstriped dungarees, thinking they would be perfect for garden time. Her mother tied her blond hair up into a bun, gave her a kiss and said, 'I'll come and bring you milk in an hour.'

With glee, Susan ran out into *her* territory, the big garden. The lush green grass stretched all the way down to the creek. Large trees created areas of dappled shade. There were colours everywhere: white and yellow roses, friendly yellow daffodils and a tall hibiscus with pink flowers as big as dinner plates. It was serene and friendly – enchanted, Susan thought.

Down by the creek she watched the sparkling water dance over the stones - a million diamonds heading to the sea.

Then she went to the roses and smelled the scent she loved. She took the time to watch a bee as it buzzed about in a busy way. 'Where do you hide your honey, Mrs Bee?' Susan asked playfully.

She loved lying under the two big pines. Grandpa had planted them fairly close together all those years ago and now, when she looked up through the channel, they seemed to point all the way to Heaven.

It was a warm day with white clouds riding across the sky like the prince's carriage in her book and after a while Susan drifted off to sleep. She dreamed that she was Princess Susan, the prettiest and kindest princess the kingdom had ever known. All the people and animals loved her.

She rode in a golden carriage that had beautiful, royal red seats, pulled by four stately white stallions with groomed manes. She looked at her clothes. Gone were the pinstriped dungarees. She was wearing a mauve dress with puffed sleeves. The sleeves, neck and hem were embroidered and edged with frilly white lace. Her crown, like the royal carriage, was gold and her blond hair hung to her shoulders.

The carriage door opened automatically and, as she stepped out, all the animals came out to welcome her with 'Hooray! Hooray!' She waved to them.

The flowers had upturned smiling faces. She had never noticed that before. The trees swayed back and forth like maidens on a Polynesian island. Even the ants stopped their toil to greet her. She seemed to float as she crossed the garden, where the reeds clutched at her smooth dress.

When she reached Snail, sitting on a big green leave, Susan saw that he was sad. 'Why are you sad, Mr Snail, when everyone else is so happy?'

'Oh, Princess Susan,' he thought, 'you are so beautiful. Why are you wasting your time talking to me?' But instead grumped, 'There is nothing wrong with me. Go and play with the others.'

'No, no, no,' Susan smiled. 'I will not let you off so easily. Now tell me what is wrong.'

'Do, do you really want to know?' he stammered, looking at the ground.

'Of course I do, that is why I am here! I am the princess of the garden and perhaps I can help you.'

'I'm sad because I'm so slow,' he said in a disgruntled way.

Susan replied, 'You are slow because you carry your beautiful cone-shaped home with you. That is so special!'

'That may be so, but everyone has something special about them,' he said. 'For instance, look at the Swallow family. They can fly and see everything. Bunny Rabbit runs so fast. And then there is Dandelion, who is as bright as the sun.' And lowering his head, he said in a sad voice, 'I don't have anything good about me.'

'That is not true. Don't you not know that everyone in the garden loves you? They all have a very warm spot for you because you are so kind and helpful.'

'I am?'

'Yes, you are. Do you not remember, when you saw some of the ants yesterday, you suggested to them that they quickly go into their nest before the summer storm came? And the day before, you helped Beetle, who was lying upside down on her shell. She was so grateful that you saved her from being embarrassed. You help others all the time.'

'It's true!' shouted Possum. 'You have helped us all at one time or another.'

'Yes, indeed,' agreed Worm.

'Have I really?' Snail said with joy. 'I did not know. I always thought that you were my friends, but I did not know that I was *your* friend too.'

'See,' Susan smiled, 'you are loved and appreciated.'

For the first time Snail lost his shyness and looked directly at Susan's face and said joyfully, 'Thank you, Princess Susan, you really are the princess of the garden.'

Susan answered, 'So that you don't ever forget how well loved you are, I am going to give you a silver trail that will forever follow wherever you have been. It will be called a love trail.'

And from that day onwards, wherever Snail went throughout the garden, he left a silver love trail behind him.

'Susan, Susan!' It was her mommy calling. 'Where are you, darling? I have milk and an apple for you.'

Opening her eyes, Susan smiled and remembered the dream. She wondered if it had been real – it had certainly *seemed* real.

As she started to get up, she saw a snail on a geranium leaf and noticed the silver love trail that glistened behind it. And she knew in her heart that the garden and all the creatures in it were more real than most people would ever understand.

Nature is the doorway

Chapter one...

Susan, in her favourite dungarees, was exploring along the stream at the bottom of the garden when she noticed a funny little man peering at her. To have a better look, she moved closer.

He was only about 15cm high and looked like a shrunken Santa Claus. He wore baggy red and white clothing, broken only by a wide black belt. His hat was long, pointed and tilted at a funny angle. Underneath the hat his face was bright and fun looking, with big red cheeks. A short white pointed beard gave him an impish look.

"Who are you?" Susan asked.

"You can't be talking to me," said the gnome in a not too impish way.

"Yes, I am" said Susan, "Why shouldn't I?"

"Because you humans have forgotten how to talk to us. In fact, if the elders knew that I was talking to you they would be angry."

"Angry," asked Susan, "Why would they get angry?"

"You humans have no consideration for anything of nature and think that you are in charge, that's why. And now I must go."

"No, please don't go," Susan pleaded in a soft and gentle voice. "I won't hurt you and only want to be your friend."

Softened by Susan's gentleness and a bit embarrassed about his outburst, the gnome said, "Ok, I'll stay, but only for a little while".

He said, "I know your name. It is Susan, isn't it?"

"Why yes, how did you know?"

In an important manner the gnome said, "We gnomes make it our business to know everything."

"A gnome! Wow! What is your name?"

"My name is Fern and I am 284 years old!"

"284", exclaimed Susan, "That's very old."

"No I'm not, I'm still young." He continued in a conspiratorial tone, "Hey Susan, you are my first human friend."

Susan's eyes sparkled and her face shone with a wide smile as she said, "Then we both have a secret, because if I told my mother and father that I could see and talk to a gnome they would not believe me."

A dove landed on the grass and busied itself eating between the blades.

"Hi Dove", said the gnome.

"Gooday Fern. Be careful, that human is pretty close and may tread on you. You know what they are like!"

"Oh, no, Susan is my friend, she is different."

"Ha, what nonsense," said Dove, extracting a particularly tasty piece of grass from the earth, "A human having respect for anything that comes from nature is unheard of." And with that the dove flew away with the morsel hanging from its beak.

Susan heard the conversation and was shocked. She started to cry. "Are we really so horrible?"

The gnome felt sorry for his friend and said, "Sadly, most are, but they have not always been like this. I remember when I was little many humans could see and talk to us, but as you moved into houses and away from nature you forgot about the folk and our connection. Once you knew that you were one with nature and all of its creatures, and understood that we are all interdependent on each other. Now men think they have sovereignty and do what they like."

A dispirited Susan asked, "That makes me feel terrible. How can I help?"

In a serious voice the gnome said, "There is only one way, and that is to bring nature back into the hearts of mankind."

Susan was thoughtful before she asked, "Can you see and talk to all the animals and creatures and can they see and talk to you?"

"Yes, we are all connected. It is only man that isn't."

"What do you mean connected?" asked Susan.

"I'm not sure if I can explain about connection as only being 284 years old, I have not that much experience. Hmmm, I wonder if I could ask Pine Cone to talk to you."
"Who is Pine Cone?"

"Oh, he is one of the elders."

"But you said the elders would be angry if they knew that you were talking to a human."
"Yes, but Pine Cone is wise and compassionate and would like to try and reach humans. Not like old Bark, the Master Elder. He is so disgruntled with humans that he thinks it would be a waste of time."

With a smile and giggle, the two friends made arrangements to meet the next day, but not before Susan bent down and gave the gnome a quick hug and kiss, saying, "I am so lucky to have you as my friend." Fern blushed and rushed away before Susan could see.

Susan wandered towards the kitchen and a biscuit. She mused, *Oh, I do like Fern. At first I thought that he was funny looking, but this is not so as he is just different. What he says about man's inconsiderate ways does worry me.*

The next day ...

Under a deep blue sky and bright sunshine, Susan ran to the stream, as she did not want to miss her friend and Mr Pine Cone. She was worried that he may not like her, but when she saw the two of them shuffling towards her, she just knew that it would be all right.

Pine Cone was shorter than Fern, but with rather a large mid section. With his arms tucked behind his back, he had a studious but comfortable look. His head was bowed towards the ground, and he occasionally nodded in an animated way as he discussed some point with Fern.

He did not wear the traditional red and white of the younger gnomes, but a formal full length coat. On his head sat a top hat. The beard was long, down to his waist, and also cut in a pointed way.

As they approached Susan, Fern said, "Excuse me Mr Cone, but here we are and there she is." Then, with formality, he said, "Mr Pine Cone, this is my friend Susan. Susan, this is Mr Cone."

Susan had never greeted a Gnome elder before and was not sure what to do. But she need not have worried, as Pine Cone gave a hearty laugh, extending his hand up towards her. "My dear, I am very pleased to meet you." He finished off with another laugh.

Susan, giggling at this friendly man, bent down and gave the hand a hearty shake. "And I am pleased to meet you Mr Cone."

"Oh, my dear, you can call me Pine if you like. Don't you think that we are too formal these days?"

"I guess so," said Susan, thinking of her father rushing to his office each day.

"Come my dear, let us sit over by the waterfall and let our friend the mist gently refresh us."
Susan daintily sat on a rock. She noticed a rainbow from the spray of the waterfall.

The elder, following her eye, said, "Do you know that the rainbow was formed by The Ancients to remind us to be grateful for water? If we did not have the Water People, we could not survive."

He seemed to be lost in thought for a little time. Then he said, "Now, this young man Fern says that you are keen to know more of the way of nature. Is that correct?"

"Yes, please."

"Well, I am willing to oblige. Where would you like to start? There is so much to talk about,"

Susan thought the discussion was to be a serious one, but Pine Cone's jovial manner made her realise that even serious topics can be approached in a playful way.

"Gee," she said, "I am not sure, but several times yesterday Fern spoke of a 'connection' and I wondered what he meant by that?"

"Good question," boomed the elder. "This is probably the most important principle for all of us. Now, when I say all of us, I mean the Gnomes and Plant Kingdom, the Fairy Folk and Divas, all the animals of the forests and plains, the Mineral Kingdom and, of course, humans."

Without pausing, the elder continued, "Yes, the connection is indeed very important. It is our link to enchantment, but it is more than that. It is the substance of our very make up." The elder paused and smiled, "Do you understand?"

"I, I think so", mumbled a hesitant Susan. "Do you mean God or something like that?"

"Yes indeedal, something like that. The Creative Essence is more present in nature than meets the eye. It has always been here. It is because of this essence that we have so much love for nature."

"Can I see it?" asked an inspired Susan.

"Of course you can, if you will only look. With perseverance little clues and hints start to emerge. You see, Susan, when you are close to nature it is easier to see the spirit that sustains us.

"Humans of the past, such as the Australian Aboriginal, the Eskimo and the Natives of America knew of this connection. They lived by it and understood its sacredness. Even now, the ancient spirits of those times try to reach man."
Susan remembered a Celtic story book that her Daddy used to read to her that talked about man and creatures living side by side.

As she thought about this, the Elder interrupted her thoughts and said, "That's right my dear, man and all the creatures knew that they were one, and that if any component of the oneness should disappear then it would affect the whole."

"How did you know what I was thinking?" asked a surprised Susan.

"Oh that," laughed the elder, "We all have telepathy. We don't really need words. Besides, the plant kingdom doesn't have mouths and so telepathy is necessary. And, indeedal, man was once able to communicate telepathically. That was before humans thought that they were superior and turned their backs on us and nature. I'm sorry, my dear, if I embarrass you, but best to tell you the truth.

"Did you know that we used to call you mankind, but as they are no longer kind we just call you collectively, man?"

Fern, who had been listening quietly, felt sorry for Susan and so lent over and gave her knee a big hug. He said, "It's okay Susan, we know that you are not like that."

"Please don't take offence," laughed the elder. "I am talking of collective humanity over the last few hundred years and not one lovely little girl with cute freckles across her nose.

"I'll bet you didn't know that we gnomes, you humans, many of the plant kingdom and all the water of the planet have much of the same mineral and trace elements, and in roughly the same proportions!

Fairy Tales

Indeedal, we are all very similar, yes very similar. But yet, there is a paradox, as, although we are from one, we are all unique.

"Now where were we? Oh yes. Man thinks that he alone has access to the intelligence of the universe. Man may have a developed brain, but the brain is not the only way to receive universal knowledge. Most knowledge is external to the brain. We Gnomes have a brain, but we only use it for everyday work. When it comes to universal or spirit connection we don't use the brain, we connect!

"Can I learn to connect?" asked an excited Susan.

"Indeedal you can, yes indeedal All it takes is a willingness to see yourself as one with the universe and keep an open and enquiring mind. By doing so, you will see that there are energetic and spiritual properties in all the creatures of nature."

After this last piece of advice, the elder stood and stretched, whilst saying, "For now, my dear girl, I think that we have talked enough for one day. I don't want to overload you, no not overload you."
"Please Mr Cone, can we meet again?" asked Susan.

"Indeedal we shall, we shall", said the elder with a chuckle. Then, folding his arms behind his back, waddled off towards the way he had come, calling, "Come, young Fern, it is time that we went on our errand to Billabank."

With that, Fern gave a quick wave to Susan as he ran after Mr. Pine Cone.

Susan sat for a while after the gnomes had gone. As if to encourage her, a lovely gold and green butterfly landed on her knee. As it rested, it rubbed its antennas together. Susan looked at the face of the butterfly and felt that she saw love and contentment. As she felt this, the butterfly rose into the air and came close to her face. For a time it floated there before fluttering towards the water for a drink.

Susan felt more at peace then, than at any time in her life.
The End.

Trees, the guardians of the soul

NATURE, ANIMALS AND EARTH

Mother Earth

I'm dying, slowly dying – yet nobody listens, nobody cares. The tragedy is not only about me. It's about all the animals that live on me, the fish in the sea, the birds, bunnies and penguins, the poor lizards and lovely beetles. All will perish with me – all species will be gone for ever.

And what about me? I have a soul and I have feelings. I don't want to die. Yet my veins are full of poisons and my air, which was once so clean and pristine, is now murky and heavy. Not to mention the toxins that have killed the goodness of my soil. The aura that surrounds me is lifeless, all the colour gone. The trees and plants are dwarfing and suffocating, dying of the same cancer as I am.

We had a deal, you and I - I would let you live here, if you respected me. Part of our deal was that you would bathe in the enchantment of what I had to offer, glory in my beauty and abundance. I am God's art.

But you have destroyed me. Like a young and innocent girl, you have whored me, brutalised me and left me to lie in my own vomit, too weak and sick to help myself. You changed the environment so what was once controlled is now out of control. Yes, it is you, man, who has caused the wind to destroy, rain to flood and sun to dry, desecrate and burn.

I cry tears of anguish for the lost future – do you not realise what you have done? How can you be so shallow in your outlook? Your law of *Thou shall not kill* is ignored when it comes to me, your mother, as every day the stake is driven deeper and the gases become more toxic. My death is slow and full of pain. I am not meant to die. Not yet, anyway. I trusted you. I did not know that you were without a soul, callous and uncompromising.

In generations to come, when I am a lifeless, barren ball of darkness, sombrely floating through the universe, the annals of history will show that man was the selfish race.

"Our scientific power has outrun our spiritual power. We have guided missiles and misguided men."
- Martin Luther King Jr., *Strength to Love*, 1963.

Nature

Farmers have a sense of it; it is unlikely that it is money keeping them on the land. Stargazers are awed in its presence. Gardeners marvel at the mystery of growth, while dirt cakes their hands and blackens their fingernails. Yet, to explain it is difficult.

The ancient tribes of the world knew it, as if it were a brother, and you can as well, if you have the intent.

I have spent many hours in the bush in both South Africa and my native Australia, a lot of time hiking and camping on my own. Always, for the first half-day, I felt alone but then I would listen and realise that I was accompanied by nature's presence. When I bedded down at night, the connection, her energy and unity, would be there.

Nature can be spectacular in her scenery but communing with nature on a deeper level is the lesson I'm referring to here. The sweet aromas of pollens and flowers after a summer storm is only a façade, as is the colour display that nature puts on for us in a field of a million poppies. As delightful as it all is, there is so much more. This is just Mother Nature's make-up, her rouge and perfume. She is like any woman, whose outside beauty does not reveal her true self. They are enticements to draw us closer - her charms to attract and seduce. Once enchanted, there is a universal desire to look deeper. Underneath her countenance, her smile, there is a depth of untold riches, to be discovered.

This union with nature is buried deep within us. Millions of people head towards the bush each weekend to experience it and many more sit on their verandas to watch, or rather feel, the sun retreat. The hikers as well as the veranda dwellers know there is something more than dazzling sunsets. But for most it is too subtle to understand, and so we are incapable of explaining it. The subconscious mind has an awareness of it but on a conscious level it eludes us. Humans flow with vibrations that are not normally felt consciously. Nature brings these closer to the surface.

Giving yourself over to nature is like sitting next to your lover and, although not talking or touching, still feeling one another's energy.

The connection is likely to be strong but, if asked to explain that force, you would find it difficult. Our language is just not rich enough. Yet you know it and knowing is the key. And so with nature, when you allow her to creep into your being, you will recognise her.

She will evoke hidden feelings of past times, when in some other form you were coupled closer to her. It is much the same as a dog barking at a full moon. He does not know why he barks but senses an affinity.

The riches that I have gained from stilling my mind and letting nature come to me are extraordinary. Like a lover, she snuggles up to me and whispers into my ear. She places thoughts in my mind, thoughts that are beneficial, never harmful, and always gentle. I have learnt much about myself through her sage advice and gained insight into universal principles. Some of my writing I can attribute to her prompting, as well as lessons in patience. But the most endearing lesson that nature has given me is humility towards herself and my role in relation to her.

Mother Nature, like a woman, wants to be wooed. She wants you to pay attention to her, to take the time, to listen and connect. When she blends into you, she will bestow all her warmth and what you will feel, and sometimes see, will be astonishing.

So take time to connect by sitting within her folds late at night when all around you are asleep. Feel the moon fall lightly into your being. Or in the day, lie under a tree, and watch the clouds scuttle across the blue sky while branches gently wave in a graceful dance. When you open to her, your mind will quieten and go beyond the silence, as you join in the rhythm of all that there is.

The Love of a Pet

He's cunning, mean and ruthless. Dog of the world that he is, he probably has all the dogs of the world within his genes. His sandy-coloured fur seems to propagate itself throughout the house, as it clings to everything he touches. He is below knee height and looks a bit like a feather duster with a shaggy tail attached at one end and a floppy-eared muzzle at the other, while four legs support the bushy undercarriage. Yogi is endowed with an amazing ability to remain puppy-like, even with the passing of many years.

Yogi believes that he is master of the house. On his canine evolutionary scale; cats are at the bottom of the chain. According to him, felines only have one brain cell and are creatures of little worth. Next are postmen and meter readers who have been put on earth for great canine sport. Female dogs are second from the top and paramount are male dogs. Yes, you guessed it, Yogi is a male dog and so all are subservient to him.

I remember the day he came into our lives. We had just collected our daughter Kim from school and there was this tiny, furry thing, about six weeks old, wandering the street and seemingly lost. Stopping the car, we called, 'Hey, doggy, come-on, doggy doggy.' Without hesitation and with an uncommon jaunt in his stride, he trotted over as if he already owned us, and scrambled into the back of the car. We cuddled him, waiting to see if a concerned owner would come looking in search of a beloved pet.

No one came. We took him home and gave him some milk, before returning to the spot to put up notices, complete with our telephone number. Over the next few days he easily settled into our lives and hearts. On the seventh day, while watching Yogi play, we looked at each other and all knew he was ours. Dressing in haste, we sped back to the notices and pulled down each and every one. That was about eleven years ago.

Yogi is crazy for dog choccies and starts his manipulations at about six in the evening. But if he gets them before eight, he forgets or pretends to forget, and commences the whining process all over again. I work from home and don't allow him into my office, so he'll wait at the entrance, doing the cute doggie thing - where a pooch lies tummy down on the floor with a dear little face resting on his two front paws that are extended in front of him, while button eyes follow his parent's every move. This is a cunning ploy meant to melt my heart. It does just that, melts my heart.

Every so often he becomes agitated and will get up and bark at me as if to say, 'Come on, man, I need my choccies,' while shuffling on the spot in frustration. Have you ever observed a dog sighing? If not, come to this house around seven any evening and you'll see what I mean.

When I finally succumb and head towards the lounge, he looks akin to someone who has just won millions in the lotto. He'll jump at my side with all the glee in the world. However, his gaze remains on me, just in case I play that rotten game of pretending to do something else. I act my part and in a childlike voice say, 'And we gonna give Yogi his choccies, because he is such a gooooood boy.'

As I open the drawer in which the goodies are stashed, he stands up on his hind legs and supports himself by placing his front paws on the drawer. Thus extended, his intelligent face peers in and supervises the proceedings as I take out the treat.

As the chronicler of his majesty's feats, I must tell you about the other dog of the realm -- Sparkleberry. According to Yogi, Sparkleberry should have been called Wimp. We were bequeathed this little madam by friends who left the country. Yogi has difficulty believing that she could have had a lineage that survived prowling the wilds ten thousand years ago in search of game to conquer and consume. But somehow her genetic pool survived and here she is. With huge marble-brown eyes that peer at you from behind daintily coiffured hair, she boasts that she is a Lhasa Apso and, judging by her behaviour, this must be a pedigree of distinction. Yogi is not impressed with her prissy demeanour and does his best to annoy her as often as possible.

Sparkleberry, on the other hand, takes none of his dominating male nonsense. She is perfectly satisfied with her real position of power in the house. 'That slob Yogi cannot even trace his lineage back one generation; in fact, the humans found him on the street and that's where he should have stayed,' she clearly thinks. She is proud of her Tibetan ancestry and imagines the good old days with fondness and pleasure.

Sparkleberry also likes her tit-bits, provided that she does not have to rouse herself to get them. Yogi thinks to Sparkleberry, 'Hey, it's choccie-drop time!'

'So, what's the panic?' she thinks back.

'Well, get up off your lazy backside and look excited!'

'The human will give me some. I don't need to be childish, not like you.'

'Yeah, yeah, you gonna miss out, that much I can tell you.'

The ritual starts with a drawled announcement, 'And here is one for Yogi.' When he hears this, his tongue salivates as it wipes his lips while he beseeches me to *get on with it!*

I pass a piece to him, which lasts just a split second. Continuing, 'And here is one for Sparkleberry,' I place one right in front of the Wimp's nose. She inspects it, like its something from Mars. You would not think that the same routine has been followed almost daily for the last five or so years!

Yogi sees this and, quick as a flash, jumps a super-dog leap of about five metres and scoops up the Wimp's drop before bouncing back to be ready for his second, or rather his third. He waits for this with his front legs supporting an upright body and eyes gleeful with delight, while his bushy tail dusts the floor as it wags from side to side. Sparkleberry looks to the ceiling and thinks, 'God, what a peasant, absolutely no manners at all.'

The score is usually four choccies to Yogi and one to The Wimp.

Let me relate the story of the grand tug-of-war. We play this game with a finished toilet-roll as the rope. I announce the sport by trumpeting through the empty holder, 'Dooodaadooooo, dooodaadooooo,' and irrespective of where Yogi is or what he is up to, he'll race through the house, full of delight and eagerness. When he arrives, his back sways to and fro because his tail is pumping at about one hundred beats per minute. Sparkleberry sighs at the boy thing and thinks, 'Boring, boring.'

To start with, Yogi will jump up like a police dog to try and savage the roll. 'Just wait my boy,' I encourage, bending down to his height to let him get a good grip with his executioner-like jaw. Then the war begins. Back and forth we cavort, up and down, like a swordfight in the swashbuckling movies of old. Yogi further intimidates his foe into submission with a fierce growl, while his head shakes from side to side in an effort to destroy the beast.

Alas, toilet rolls are destructible and so, with a final rip, the two sides separate. At this stage the wily canine indicates that yet again he has won and, complete with his soggy kill, triumphantly trots away to settle down to tearing it up into a million pieces.

We arrive at the end of Yogi's day. His choccies were consumed about an hour ago and the gas heater replaces the winter cold with pleasant comfort. Sparkleberry is asleep in her basket and Yogi, lying next to me, his head on my lap, is dreaming doggy dreams - he is the leader of a fierce pack of killer dogs, his fur flattened with the speed of the chase, while his foaming muzzle emits a bloodcurdling challenge to the following pack as the scent of the hunt in his nostrils drives him faster and faster.

Yogi is now gone, but if you liked Yogi, see my book; **Yogi, the tails and teachings of a suburban alpha doggy**.

Life lessons

Life Lessons are the soul's way of helping you identify areas of personal growth and have a major influence on life. They also indicate an aspect of life that needs change in some way. If you listen to the lesson and adjust (with trust) things will flow better.

'These lessons are the windstorms of life, they make us who we are.'
Elisabeth Kubler-Ross

You incarnate to grow and learn, and so arrive with specific lessons to master. These usually govern major influences of your life, such as; unconditional love, trust (in the creator) or overcoming fear. **Each lesson that you overcome helps to balance you with the flow of life**. Conversely, lessons not mastered are a block to the flow of life, as well as a block to your abundance. Throughout life, you will have several major and numerous smaller lessons.

As you are to grow closer source, it is imperative to remain balanced. When not balanced you are separate from Source. To align, you are given messages. At first, these are subtle, but if they go unheeded they get louder and firmer. Many choose to ignore these messages until such time as disease, accident, retrenchment or other problems force you to acknowledge them.

I have a friend whom I shall call Sue. Sue was the youngest of 5 siblings and from an early age was told to, 'Shut up Sue, what do you know?' The consequence was that she felt inadequate whenever it came to formal conversation. She had the image of, '**I am not good at formal conversation.**' Her life lesson was to overcome this image. To support this, her soul offered opportunities to contribute to conversations, especially business conversations But each time her low self esteem kicked in and she would freeze. For over 40 years she ignored the lesson and so developed a jaw deformity. This was to such a degree that it required major surgery.

In summary, Sue developed a life lesson, as a result her soul gave her many opportunities to address the lesson. By not attending to these, the prompting got sterner, until she was given a very vivid symbolic gesture (ironically the operation could only have treated the symptom and not the cause. Only Sue is able treat the cause).

Here are some guidelines that apply to life lessons:
- A life with unresolved lessons, is a difficult life
- You are never given a life lesson that you cannot handle
- What you don't finish in this life follows you to the next
- Ascension is not likely to happen if you have unresolved life lessons

When a life lesson is learnt and mastered, it does not mean that your life automatically becomes perfect, but it does mean a smoother ride.

Learning life lessons means taking responsibility, and by doing so you learn more about the hidden part of you. Whereas, not resolving lessons means that you remain ignorant of your shadow side.

The thought of Life Lessons may seem a bit daunting, so a good way to soften the term is by calling them 'soul-nudges'. Think of soul-nudges as an in built empowerment tool.

Elephant Walk

The shadows cast by my family on the dry soil are small and squat as the midday sun shimmers down on their backs.

I keep a watch on the herd, worrying about their safety. As the patriarch I must set an example and try to bring cheer to the young ones.

We walk towards the higher ground, where it will be cooler, and where new green succulent trees are waiting to be eaten. My mind tells them (infrasonic) stories of times past. But the young ones are clever and get angry. 'Why are those days gone? Why can't we migrate beyond this area and meet in our hundreds as we have done for generations? We, the young bulls will stand and fight and reclaim what is ours!'

I ignore the youthful aggression and continue to pass on the lore, as it was passed on to me some fifty seasons ago – the lore and stories that have been told for eons.

We come to a stream, where I have bathed for as long as I can remember. But where it was once wide and full, it is now just a trickle, the sweet taste gone, replaced with a sour smell. Man, yes once again, it is man who has done this.

I recall Ganoon, my little brother, as he sucked in a large amount of water from this very stream. When I looked up, he squirted it in my face. How could I be angry when I saw the fun in his eyes? And now a tear leaves mine as I remember how he dropped in pain and confusion at a poacher's thunder.

My sadness is interrupted by Han, our youngest cow, just out of nursing. 'How far is it to the top, Father? I'm getting tired.'

'Not far, sweet child, it will not be long before you taste those delectable leaves.' I don't tell her that there are some just over the hill, but we are stopped by man's stinging fence. I do however, remind her that her name means bright eyes; it makes her happy.

I let the young ones play for a while longer, as the climbing gets tougher. Besides, it will be cooler if we wait a bit.

Bits and Pieces

It is Zedda who comes across and says, 'I can feel you are remorseful about things past and present. Be strong, my Bull, as the rest draw direction from you.'

'Ah Zedda, you have always been my best-loved cow. You know me well.'

'I know you well because I have journeyed with you for many seasons. I have felt you shuddering inside me as you planted your seed, and I have carried your children. You are wise and caring – yes, I know you well.'

'How can I not despair for our race? Man pens us in and stops us from roaming the plains of our heritage – there is less food and water and man grows more in number all the time. Where will it end? Each season they make it harder for us.'

'My Bull, this is not your fault. You have no control over the destruction wrought by man. It is not only our species that is hurt, it is all of nature. Look at what they have done to the rivers, the air and some of our brother animals. You, our leader, must remain clear-headed.'

I flap my ears to help cool me down and say, 'You are right, but it seems that we of the elephant species suffer more than others. I fear that the man-bird, with the wings that go around in circles above its head and the call of 'woh, woh, woh', will come. Because when it does, it leaves half of our loved ones dead. As we have a season for birthing, there is a season for killing, and this is the season.'

Zedda thinks to me in pain, 'I can't fathom a race that butchers, but not for food. They seem to have no understanding of the spirit of things.'

I say nothing, as there is nothing to say and then tell her, 'We must be on our way. Go and call the others and head towards the heavy tree valley. I will bring up the rear.'

As we walk, our minds transfer directions and warnings. We tell one another stories and we tease the younger ones for not being able to walk with a graceful swing. I think to them, 'We are the biggest animal of the bush, but must walk with the silence of a snake.'

Trees, the guardians of the soul

Bits and Pieces

On the surface all is fun as we cover the ground, ground that has been walked by our forefathers. But I know that it will soon happen, I can feel it. Oh, there is no sign other than the one in my heart, but I know. Yet I am powerless to stop it from happening. There is nowhere we can hide from that vulture-like man-bird, as it knows our habits.

By late afternoon, with the low sun stretching the shadows, it is cooler. We don't have far to go. I can smell those leaves and think encouragement to the others.

'Out of my way,' Han chirps to the group, 'I want to eat first.'

Preen, a young bull, laughs. 'No, little one with bright eyes, you must wait for your elders to have the first tasting.'

'Woh, woh, woh,' reaches my ears.

Knowing that they'll be upon us very soon, I trumpet alarm, 'Hurry!' and take off myself in panic. 'No, please no, don't kill my family,' I think.

We all run fast and furiously as the 'woh, woh, woh' gets closer and louder.

'Run, Han, the man-bird comes!'

'Why do they want to hurt us, Father? We don't hurt them!'

'Run child, run!' is all I can answer.

Everything is a blur of passing trees and rocks, while the drumming of our legs hitting the ground can be felt and heard for miles.

As I catch Zedda, I see the man-bird come over the ridge. It starts to circle us, like the lion, before it pounces.

'Faster Zedda, it is here.'

'I can't, my Bull. I am old and not strong any more. You take the others and I will do my best to keep up.'

As she says this, the man-bird thunder cracks and blood instantly spurts from behind Zedda's ear. She collapses and is gone from me.

Trees, the guardians of the soul

Bits and Pieces

Tears wash my eyes and pain stings my heart, but I must continue to protect my family.

The thunder cracks again and Han, my youngest and dearest, stumbles and falls. I have to stop to be with my child.

'Father,' she thinks to me, 'it hurts. I need your touch - please touch my trunk with your trunk. Father, things are getting bleary, I can't see you – are you touching me, Father? Are you ...?' And the thunder hits me.

I stand there, determined to defy them, 'You will not kill me.' But with my strength kicked out of me, I collapse onto my front knees. 'I must get up and save my herd,' I think desperately, but the bush whirls around me as my body folds to the ground. For a moment, I lie there knowing that my life is seeping out of me and into the dusty ground. While I still have strength, I plead: 'Please God, look after our loved ones!'

Say _NO_ to culling!!!

Bits and Pieces

The Yippee Story (set in the USA)

Salmon: I'm drowning, my gills can't breathe. Will these waterfalls ever end? I must have leapt a thousand or more times.

Angel Narrator: Does the salmon's swimming against the rapids feel like *your* life?

Salmon: One day I'm enjoying myself in a tranquil bay in the sea and suddenly I get this urge to leave and swim upstream. Why did I do this? It just does not make sense, heeding a call to seek something that I don't even understand.

Angel Narrator: There is always a gentle push from God to get you to know it.

Salmon: Yet I'm not on my own, there are thousands of us. Well, there were when we started. Many have given up or been left along the way.

Whew, I'm tired, I think I'll just rest in this backwater for a mo. Oh, there's Goia. Wonder how he is doing?

"Hey Goia, how you doin?"

"Hi Fenis, I'm bushed. Why are we doing all this upstream work, searching for who knows what?"

"Beats me Goia, but it must be good for the call to be so strong."

Angel Narrator: No, you don't really know what you are looking for. But when you find it, you will know it.

Salmon: "Do you think that we are going in the right direction?"

"Who knows, Goia, we have certainly passed many side streams and perhaps any one of those may have been the direction. Something seems to be guiding us. Guess we just have to trust."

Trees, the guardians of the soul

Angel Narrator: Sometimes you do go in the wrong direction, but you'll always be gently guided back to the right path – that is, provided you listen. And, like the salmon, you also must learn to trust.

Salmon: "Well we had better continue 'our journey'. Let's head this way."

Some time later …

Salmon: "Boy, Goia the stream is certainly strong here, I'm using all my strength and don't seem to be getting anywhere."

Angel Narrator: Yes, it can get tough finding your way, very tough indeed. And sometimes there seems to be no logic to it, your entire world is turned topsy-turvy. As I said, you have to continue in trust. Besides, what alternative do you have?

Salmon: "Goia, did you hear me, where are you? Goia, are you dropping back?"

"You go on, Fenis, I, I can't go any further – I am too tired and I need to rest for a while."

"No, Goia, don't give up. By doing that all your hard work would have been wasted. Goia, do you hear me?"

Angel Narrator: No effort put into finding your Source is ever wasted. The goal, however, is only attained once you reach your destination.

Salmon: Poor Gioa, perhaps he will be OK. Wish I could help him but only he can do it for himself. I must be all the more determined and swim harder.

Angel Narrator: Unlike the salmon, sometimes it is easier to get to the Higher Power when you let go and don't try so hard. The connection has always been there, but in your business you cannot see it.

Bits and Pieces

Salmon: Hey, I'm feeling better now and, somehow different. I wonder if I am getting closer to what I am meant to find?

Angel Narrator: As you get closer, you will also feel different. You will be happier and more balanced.

Salmon: Over there, I must go over there. Yes, this feels right, this is the place. Wonder what I am to do now that I am here?

Hey, what's going on? Something inside me feels very strange, strange but nice. What are those millions of bubbles that are coming out of me? Yes, this is my purpose – I feel wonderful, yippee.

Angel Narrator: You will also feel like shouting for joy and it will seem as if you are releasing a million coloured balloons.

Remember no matter how tough your journey may seem, we will always be with you, and once you reach your purpose we will also shout yippee.

BITS AND PIECES

Africa

It is more so in this land than in any other that a man can hand another his dignity, or trample on it. Which do you do? Africa is a land of contrasts; beauty and filth are seen in the same image, as are poverty and grace, bigotry, suspicion and charity.

It is God's breeding ground for love or hate, fear or hope, where the law of the jungle prevails as one animal eats another to survive. It s also the law of some of Africa's people. Yet there are also those with the highest ideals, people with gratitude in their hearts and hope in their minds.

The opposite of love is fear and we are meant to transcend it, to live in trust that God will look after us, and is there not a better place than Africa to confront those fears. This patch of motherland is one where our fear is most often aroused.

Remember that life is a mirror that reflects the truth of who you are and Africa magnifies that truth. Are you loving or hateful, resentful or compassionate, living in fear or in trust?

It is in Africa that your charitable nature is revealed. You either give to the beggar with a generous heart or withhold in non-acceptance. It is here that you express the love that is inherently within you or is repressed without compassion. Search your heart.

Many have been beaten and savaged by the hand of Africa and know of its harshness, always ready to invoke the weakness that resides within us, to let fear be dominant.

It is in this domain that we can be full of forgiveness or loathing. A forgiving nature tells you a lot about the spiritual connectedness of a human. Where do you stand? Do you forgive or loathe?

Yet, Africa is also a place of beauty and happy faces, faces that are bright with hope and joy, faces that express the simplicity of a race closely connected to nature.

Bits and Pieces

Yes, Africa will expose you. It will reveal your spiritual development. It is here that we must look within and discover how spiritually developed we are.

It is easy to live in a land of calm and plenty, where society is ordered and regulated and respect is plentiful. But Africa offers us a chance to live our truth. We are blessed to be here and to be propelled on our spiritual journey because of its beautiful but chaotic climate.

Bits and Pieces

Who am I

"Who are you?" crooned the caterpillar.

Alice replied rather shyly, "I – I hardly know. I know who I was when I got up this morning, but I think I must have changed several times since then." (from Alice in Wonderland by Lewis Carroll)

"Who are you?" you ask *of* me.

"Like Alice, I hardly know, perhaps a constellation of a million personalities, or a thousand inconsistent moods. How can I know who I am?"

"Just like everyone, I laugh and cry and make mistakes, mistakes that I have made over and over again."

"You are a writer,' some may say, 'with published works.'"

"No, that is not me, not the real me. Writing is something that I do to try and make sense of the world."

"What about an entrepreneur?" you offer.

"Yes, I suppose I am. Some find their persona in their work and announce with obvious importance, *I am an accountant'*, or *an academic* and show you this by carrying a sheaf of impressive looking papers under a bent arm.

Although I enjoy my various vocations, I am *not* my work. After all, it is not the work that counts, but who the person is.

Hmmm, who am I? Yes that question has been asked by humanity since humanity was able to form thoughts.

Certainly by asking who I am, you are trying to put a label on me and reduce my potential. Would it not be better to ask me, *who am I not?*

Trees, the guardians of the soul

However, I do get an inkling as to who I am when I hush my mind and connect to my inner self. Only then does my core start to emerge.
Or when I go outside and stand under a tree and feel the greatness of Mother Nature, or stare in awe at an ink-black starry night. In these moments it is easy, but, when lost in day to day activity and the clutter of life, I don't know who I am.

Now, it is my turn to be the caterpillar and ask *you*, do you know *who you* are?"

A Tribute

Twenty-two years ago I knew nothing about management, and it was with trepidation that I applied to the University of the Witwatersrand Business School in Johannesburg, South Africa, to study their 'Management Advancement Program', known as MAP. Map is considered by some to be a mini MBA.

My trepidation was a result of being hopelessly dyslexic. It had forced me to leave school at the legal age of sixteen, almost illiterate.

Somehow I was accepted for the course. But at the induction speech my concerns heightened when it was announced that, *out of 102 of you, 99 have a degree.*

I looked around to see if I could spot the other 'non-degreed' persons and wondered if there were some tell tale signs, such as animated arrows, pointing at us.

It was fine for the first few months, attending lectures, taking notes and doing home study. At that stage the syndicate work had not started and assignments were typed on a PC. So my unintelligible scrawl did not come under scrutiny.

This, however, was short lived, as the first set of exams rushed forth to expose me. I knew that I knew the work, but could I convey that knowledge in my long hand, or was it rough hand?

Into the first exam I went and it was all too soon that the professor announced, "Time's up". I looked at my paper, the one that appeared to have been written by a 6 year old, and handed it in with a sinking feeling.

"Well, that is the end of that", I announced when I got home. "There is no way that they will allow me to continue," I moaned.

My wife suggested that I go and tell them that I am dyslexic. "After all, what have you got to lose?" she prodded.

And so I made an appointment with the course convenor to lay bare my dilemma. At the appointed time I was ushered into his office. He was short and kindly looking and asked in a gentle English accent, "What can I do for you, young man?"

Fearing the worst, I told him that I had neglected to inform them that I am dyslexic, and, as a result, presumably out of my depth. My eyes were downcast as I apologised.

As he spoke I looked up at him and saw an encouraging smile. I will never forget his words. "Dyslexic you say, do you think that we did not know?" At this stage his smile broadened.
"Of course from your assignments and exam it was obvious. But don't worry. We are looking for understanding of the course content, not academic excellence." He then picked up a file that was obviously mine. Whilst browsing he continued, "Hmmm, I see that you have been marked with 61%. Congratulations, you have passed."

I don't remember what I mumbled, but before long he chuckled and said with mirth, "Oh yes, the professor did admit that he had a torrid time deciphering the paper. If fact, you may have had a better mark except for the fact that there were some sections which he simply could not fathom."

I floated out of there on cloud nine. For the first time in my life, my handicap had not blocked me.

Proudly the following year I received my university diploma, after having passed all eight modules.

How different it could have been was it not for that man and his policy. I entered as a sparrow and leaft as an eagle!

Many times over those 22 years I have thought and spoken of that decisive time in my life. And each time I have remembered the gentle and kind manner in which his words were spoken. Yet, for a time, his name went out of my mind.

Bits and Pieces

Without realising it, I met him two years ago when I joined a writers' group. When I did, there was a familiarity about him that I could not recollect.

One day, whilst talking to the chair person, she mentioned her involvement in MAP as a lecturer. I told her that I had done MAP and had been in the second intake. "Well," she said, "You probably dealt with Walter Murton?" It was then that the penny finally rolled down the slot and I put the face and the name together with that of the understanding educator – it was indeed Walter Murton.

Footnote
Unfortunately the realisation came some 4 months after Walter's death. After writing this dedication, I read it to his wife Joan. Although it was over the phone, I could sense the tears and hear the sniffles as she said with a mixture of joy, pride and sadness, "Yes, Walter was like that."

Box Processor

The party hummed with the blending of many voices. Background music added to the din.

Earlier I had told her that I was a bus driver. I did this to see if her interest in me would wane. It did.

Later, I was caught out, and she asked aggressively, 'Why did you say you were a bus driver when you are in the software industry?'

I told her, 'People usually us ask what we do with the intention of processing us, to put us into the correct box and to judge whether we are worthy of their time. Most people don't make the effort to see people for who they really are. They would be better off trying to access our character and getting a feel for us first.'

'Fuck you,' she said, before she stormed off.

I wondered if she was annoyed with me for misleading her or because she was caught out as a box processor!

Dweller in the Innermost

The search for the dweller of our innermost part can be a search of extraordinary fun - a peek at all of those things hidden in our minds - you know that thing that we think we think with.

It does not necessarily have to be a serious pursuit, as most seem to believe. Make it resemble an Easter egg hunt, a search of delight, anticipating the next find, like discovering the elusive fragment from a 1500-piece jigsaw puzzle. We look to see what makes us tick or why we tock that way.

And so the clever dweller in the innermost will not take the hunt too seriously, otherwise he will get lost in most of the inner and that is not fun. It can be dark in there, a slum of sorts.

When you open the door of this Pandora's Box, you are likely to find all sorts of junk. Go on - climb in and squirm through the debris of a lifetime. Some of it is worthwhile, but most is just stuff that has gathered dust, and is ready to be put out with the garbage.

It is only when you find the Easter eggs of your search that will you start to get an inkling of the power of *the dweller within*.

This short text was inspired by GF Watt's Dweller in the Innermost. *He lived from 1817 to 1904.*

It's All Perfect

Hannah stared at the floor, disbelieving, thinking now what? Her normally tranquil face showed sadness. But, becoming philosophical, she said to Martin, 'Look, it's his lesson. He knows as well as anyone that stealing is against Universal principles. I think he took the money because by doing so he's perpetuating a belief that he's worthless.'

Martin was agitated and patrolled the room like a secretary bird in search of food. He said, 'Perhaps, but that doesn't help us. It's annoying to think of the time and effort it took to earn it, just for him to blow it on drugs and booze. Besides which, how are we now to pay the builders for the new wing?'

Hannah, her hands gently resting in her lap, calmly answered, 'Well, we will just have to put it out to God for a solution. If we trust, He will supply.'

Martin said, 'I hope so, but *His time* does not always equate to *our time*.'

'Have trust, Martin; has He ever let us down?' But then she added with concern, 'I feel sorry for Ashley. His demons are too much for him and I fear they may drive him to destruction.'

While thinking, Martin adjusted the squeegee that held his ponytail in place, 'If he returns, I'll kick him out of the house.'

Hannah, watching Martin closely, knew that when he fiddled with his hair his mind was usually working overtime. She said gently, 'Relax, Martin; everything happens for a reason. Ashley's mindset is one of fear, ours is of compassion. Let it go, and focus on the now.'

Martin loved his wife and felt her wisdom seep into him. He looked at her sitting in the chair, poised and relaxed, and said, 'I wish I could be more like you - living your belief as you do. I just can't prevent myself from taking things personally.'

Smiling, she said, 'The path is perfect, irrespective of where we are on it,' and as an afterthought added, 'and so is Ashley's.'

Bits and Pieces

Martin sat down and thought about Ashley. His progress had been good and he was trying to clean himself up. Perhaps it was the dark side asserting itself, one last time. Martin knew that if Ashley returned he would forgive him or at least pretend to forgive him. Otherwise all the teachings would be a lie.

A knock at the door caught their attention. It was Ashley, sporting a sheepish grin, a lock of hair hanging over his eyes. As he entered the room he said, 'I thought I had better return the rest of this before I blew it.' His blue jeans, supported by a wide belt and buckle, were filthy, as was his windbreaker. 'Sorry, I used some of the money but most of it is here. I will pay you back by working at the market, if that's OK?'

Martin looked at Hannah and saw her knowing smile light up her face.

My Brother John (a true story)

It was only years later that I ascribed my daydreaming to the German who used to lock me in the dunny for hours on end.

Dunny is a lovely Australian word, meaning an outside toilet. This dunny, like all dunnys of the period, was a small hut, invariably made with wooden slats and a tin roof. All seemed to have rickety doors and spider webs in the corners. Dunnies were far enough away from the house so that an incoming breeze would not spoil meals. Yet not so far that it was a trek - who wants to wake up at night, in the middle of winter, and traipse kilometres up the garden?

Yes, after Mom absconded, Dad left my brother and me in the not too good care of a countryman of his. I call him the German because, as I was only three at the time, I cannot remember his name. So we stayed with him and his family on their farm out in the back part of Sydney.

The German did not like me and took great delight in demonstrating this. One of his favourite pastimes was to lock me in the dunny whenever he went out. While I was incarcerated, my brother John was given strict instructions not to let me out - otherwise he would regret it. Knowing the German, John was too petrified to buck the command.

I remember one such time; perhaps it was not just one time but all the times that a small child rolls into one. I must have sat in that box all day. To start with, slithers of sunlight shone through the slats from behind me. Many daydreams later, they were in my face, with dust particles dancing in the shafts of light.

I sat on the closed seat as otherwise, being just a little thing, I would have fallen in. The wood became hard after a while and hurt my bum. Of course, there was no food and no water. I don't recall what went through my mind as the hours passed. I do, however, remember my brother. Not once would he leave my side or rather, the side of the dunny. If I was about three he would have been five. We did not talk, as he was the silent type. But, if suddenly I would say, 'John, are yer there?' there would always be the reassuring answer, 'Yeah.' His support was my solace.

Bits and Pieces

Two hours later: 'John, yar there?' 'Yeah Pat, I are'. He never wandered away or faltered in his vigilance to support his little brother. How my five-year-old brother took on this duty I will never know, but I'll always be grateful. As an adult reflecting on it, I think that in many ways, John's burden was worse than mine.

These memories are my earliest and probably stick because of their profundity.

A year or so later, it was John who supported me while we were in the orphanage. He was my personal guardian angel, always there, not saying much but always a strong presence.

More years passed and he was still there, a silent support system. We grew up and how sad I was when the day came, and as a man of fifteen my brother John joined the navy. He was heading to the other side of the country, some 3500 kilometres away.

Now, 42 years later, I still feel the tears prickling my eyes when I recall John aboard a train, called *The Spirit of Australia,* as it detached itself from the station and pulled him ever faster away from me.

Palms – A Natural Biography

The palms of my hands chart my life of events. Events of joy and sadness, success, failure, loves, hopes, hurts and fears.

Resembling spider-webbed lines, with lumps and striations, blemishes, like a parched river pan - a biography of fornications and drunken exploits, of friends, compassion, children raised, of love, sweet romances, brutality, brawls, tranquillity, regrets, arguments, anger, attitudes and addictions, optimism and happiness – all are represented.

Although my palms are cluttered and packed like an over-stocked graveyard, I revel in thoughts of lines to come and thrill in the prospect of new etchings.

After all, an unblemished palm would indeed reveal a boring life.

Southern Cross

Sitting on the veranda, I stared at her last resting place. The memories came, as did the tears. After I had buried her, I left to recover, but later returned to build and develop our land. That was many years ago.

In my short time away, the farm had started to return to the bush from whence it came. The grass was longer and the animals had claimed what was once theirs. The Kangaroos had eaten all that the garden offered and had trampled some of the fences. Alone, I set to work with an almost manic will.

We had met on board the *King James* en route to Tasmania. We were both immigrating, she involuntarily, as she was one of fifty-eight female prisoners. Her crime was the theft of vegetables, for which she was sentenced to be transported to the penal colony in Tasmania.

I was a fare-paying passenger, a 'free settler' – not so much wanting to go to Australia, as I knew very little about the place, but wanting to escape the poverty and harshness of Manchester. My father had died as a result of overwork and the terrible conditions in the textile factories. Two years of that toil was enough for me.

The year was 1845. I was seventeen years old and heading to a new life.

I first saw her when she and some of the other prisoners had some deck time; I was watching them and wondering what their lot was likely to be in the colony. Suddenly she looked up and our eyes met. Neither of us found it uncomfortable; it seemed very natural. I was too far away to make out the colour of her eyes but close enough to get a sense of her. She was of small frame and regal in her bearing; she stood upright and strong like a willow in full leaf.

The *King James* was a converted tea trader ship that used to do the run from China to England before the discovery of wild tea in India, when the Chinese tea trade came to an end. She was one hundred and ninety one feet in length with a registered tonnage of seven hundred and ninety-nine tons. She would have been well suited for those fascinating races from China to England with the first tea of the season, as she was particularly fast in a light breeze. The hold had been converted to house the prisoners.

We left the busy port of Southampton for Hobart Town in Tasmania, where I was hoping to take a position on a farm for a year or so. As a free settler, I was entitled to a grant of land. I knew nothing of farming, but was willing to learn. Anything would be better than slaving fifteen hours a day in industrial England.

We had a dream crossing, in a record time of twenty-two days, not the twenty-nine it usually took. There were no storms, just a fair breeze at our backs. Nor was there death from scurvy, for which most of the trips were notorious.

I took notice when the prisoners were allowed on deck. I learnt that her name was Megan and that even in incarceration she was the most serene person I had ever seen. Her calm face always radiated a warm smile. Others must have felt it as well for she was forever surrounded by a posse of transportees.

The day we arrived in Hobart is a day I will never forget. It was early in the afternoon when the Master called, 'Land ho, land ho!'

It was an exhilarating time and everyone, including the prisoners, who were all on deck to see the new land. The summer sun was silver in the deep blue sky. White billowing clouds were scattered across the vista, like sheep in a blue paddock, and sea eagles glided around the *King James* in hope of scraps. We could see the harbour with Mount Wellington standing proud and strong in the background.

Excitement filled the air, an expectation of a new life to come. I found myself standing next to her. We looked at each other and she smiled, a smile that was deeper than the sea we skipped over, and held as much promise as the country with which we were soon to merge. There were no words between us, as the prisoners were not allowed to talk to free settlers, but it seemed almost prophetic that we shared this moment together.

The *King James* docked at Hobart Town, where Megan was assigned to the service of Warden Graham's family. Warden Graham was in charge of the penal colony in Port Arthur. I found work as a farm hand some twenty miles from Hobart Town.

Megan took part in the Graham family's trips to Hobart, where the Warden went on business while his wife shopped for supplies and enjoyed social contacts. It was on one such visit that I almost knocked Megan over in a general dealer's store. She, by then, had gained the trust of her custodians and had a certain amount of freedom to purchase supplies for the family. I apologised and timidly asked her, 'How much time do you have left?'

She replied, 'Eighteen months.' It was the first time that I had heard her voice. It had the same serene quality as her appearance, not frightened or aggressive but soft and firm. Her eyes, steel grey, searched my face as if confirming something she already knew. A gentle smile came to her face as she asked me my name. 'Joseph White,' I replied.

Eighteen months later we were married.

In 1847 I obtained the grant to which I was entitled. And so, with a small dowry and the good wishes of the Warden and his family, we were on our way.

The grant was further north on the East Coast of Tasmania in the Bicheno area, some hundred and five miles from Hobart Town. It had reasonable water and good agricultural potential. I built a simple stone house of two rooms with a dirt floor and a new straw roof that kept out the rain and heat of summer, but made it cosy in the bitterly cold winters. Megan worked the garden to provide food for the table. We supplemented this with meat from the abundant game that the land supplied.

Working side by side from sunup to sunset, we fenced and cleared the grant. On summer nights we would take out blankets and make love under a ceiling of a million stars. Afterwards we played games by making out shapes in the Milky Way. Megan's favourite was the Southern Cross, a small constellation of five stars. 'Just like us,' she would say, 'on our own and separate from the main clutter of humanity. Naturally we named the farm *The Southern Cross*.

Sometimes we slept outside all night and would be woken by the thump, thump, thump on the ground as wallabies bounced past. Galahs screeched in the dawn, while crows flapped overhead, their throaty squeals creating a racket fit to waken the dead. I would rise first to get the fire going and boil the tea. The fragrant eucalyptus burnt, and sent wisps of smoke into the early light. At peace, I would sit and watch the sun glimmer through the gum trees as it rose.

The farm was making progress and supplied most of what we required. We did not need much; we had each other and the bush, a place that teemed with life. Occasionally we would go down to Swansea, some fifteen miles away, for supplies and news. But we were so self-sufficient that we would be glad to return to our own little corner of the world.

Then there was a flash flood upstream. We did not know that several head of cattle had been trapped and drowned. Their carcasses rotted in the stream and contaminated our drinking water.

I was working in the garden when I felt the first sharp stabs of a headache and a deep weariness enveloped me. It was not long before the sweating started, followed by nausea. I don't know for how long Megan nursed me; it could have been ten or twelve days. In lucid periods between bouts of delirium, I could see that she was always at my side, washing me down to lower my temperature, spoon-feeding me vegetable broth or pouring water onto a cloth to drip into my mouth. I did not know it at the time but the fever was in her as well.

Upon recovering, I called for her, but there was no reply. Perhaps she is outside, I thought. In time I called again, 'Megs Darling!' as loudly as my strength allowed. Collapsing back in weariness I slept some more.

When I woke, the afternoon sun shone through the west window and I could see dust particles floating in the air like ripples on sparkling water. 'Megan!' I called. After a few minutes I became worried and pulled myself up. It was then that I saw her on the floor. She was in her work clothes and apron and in her hand she still held the cloth she had used to quench my thirst.

Scrambling over to her as quickly as my weak body would allow, I could not help my moan, 'No, please, no.' I knelt down and cradled her head in my lap. Megan opened her eyes and smiled at me. Weakly she held out her hand and caressed my face. She tried to say something, but the words would not come out.

It was only when she knew that I had recovered that she gave in to the fever. The smile froze on her face and her hand dropped to the floor as she died. Numbness filled my mind and for a period all time ceased to exist.

Sitting on the veranda, I remembered our first and only argument. It was after a blistering hot day when the bush was so still that it looked like a frameless painting. We bickered about where to place the front gate. I wanted the most direct route. She felt it should come in from the north quarter where it would run through the grove of gums, to sort of sneak up on the house over the rise. I muttered that she spoke rubbish.

It was some time later, when I was down by the stream brooding over what had happened, that I felt her soft touch on my back. She said, 'I am sorry, my love. I have failed you and made you angry, but in the process I have also hurt myself. Let's let the flower of our love forever smile on us as we treat one another with the respect of our love.'

I grabbed her and held her tight in gratitude for her wisdom and strength. The gate was put where she suggested, as it was a magnificent approach to the farm. I looked at it now and saw the shrubs flowering that I had planted in her memory.

As weak as I was, I had had no problem carrying her emaciated body to the pump. Taking the cloth, I washed her down, all the time shaking in remorse. A passage in the bible came to my mind, from Corinthians, 'Love is not resentful.' This gave me strength enough to continue. But the pain was deep and tears poured down my cheeks and splashed on her forever-placid face.

Even now I wonder, why did she not let me know of her sickness? Somehow we could have helped each other. I know that her answer would have been: for selfless love. She would have made the decision in love and the hope that I would live. That is what would have been important to her. So I lived while she died.

She had the ability to love deeply and naturally – to give herself totally, without expecting or wanting anything in return. Her faith in life and nature and a belief in a benevolent creator gave her a feeling of oneness with the universe in which she lived. It was for this reason that she loved this land - as harsh as it was. She felt she was part of it, as if the trees had buried their roots in her being as well as in the ground. The wild animals had a sense of her soul and did not show any fear at her approach. The wind was her breath and the dust her perfume.

She understood the cycles of life and the oneness of all, and that death would also be birth in another form. Her body would fertilise the ground, ensuring rounds of further seasons, where she would return in the wind. I knew she loved life, and me, but her sacrifice would not have been a sacrifice in her mind; it would have been an expression of love and giving. Yes, she would have liked to have lived - to see the fruits of the farm and the changing of the seasons, and perhaps a child or two running around.

Twenty-two years later, the farm is productive and the kids are away at boarding school. Jenny is in the kitchen cooking dinner. And although I am at peace there is not a day that I do not think of Megan. How could I not? I feel her in the trees and the wind whispers her love. I look at the spot below the gum tree where we used to lie and remember as if it were yesterday.

The Initiation
Understanding Experience

The buffalo strip ripped his skin, and blood seeped out of wounds that had stretched and festered. With pain tugging at his consciousness, White Feather did not know reality from dream. Yet he did not yield to it or to the tiredness.

It seemed like years ago that he had arrived from the city to the flat expanse of the reservation. Stepping out of his jeans and windbreaker, he had merged into a world that was far removed from stress and noise, a world of ancestors and truth, where culture and spirit are one.

This was his home and at thirty-six he came to meet himself and to learn lessons.

Leapfrogging time dragged and raced with flashing images enmeshed in delirium and mixed emotions: sad, euphoric, puzzled, regretful, loving, hating; all to be worked through, continually searching for wisdom and, in doing so, the hope of finding his soul.

Experience is what you get on the way to death, so use it and gain by it. You can't buy it, yet there is a cost as re-learning is expensive. Nor can we swap experience or receive it on a platter.

This seemed to be the theme that came from his higher self. It spoke of embracing the teaching of experience. Into the future he saw that he was to be a leader and that wisdom was to be within his mind, and so over the days and nights that followed, understanding came.

The blood-stained leather thong was embedded into slits in his skin, woven like a basket, the other end attached to the top of the totem pole. This tether was not long enough to allow him to seek the comfort of the ground and so forced him to stand or rotate around the pole in endless circles. There was no respite; if he slumped, the weight of his body stretched the leather and tore the skin. In years to come, his scars would bear testimony to his search for truth.

His ancestors continued to teach: *Elders and parents try to pass experience on to the young; and they generally ignore it. Somehow it is intuitively known that they must gain their own schooling firsthand, to have it from the inside.* Through a clouded mind he wondered: *Why is direct experience so important?* In lucid moments he pondered that perhaps this understanding comes from past lives and knowing your own experience. *Is this the reason why we have past lives, to give us knowing? After all, in theory, God could simply have filled our heads with movie-type experiences. But he didn't.*

Deep into the second night, in answer to the question, with cold rain pounding the back of his bowed head, he saw an image: *a time when, as a child, euphoric and feeling warrior-like after shooting his first antelope, he experienced the joy of speeding young legs to the kill. Then abruptly, tears flooded his eyes and rolled down his cheek as he saw what he had done. His heart exploded in his chest with a grief that has never left him.*

He was guided to know the pain and those first flushes of joy. 'Feel it,' he was told. *He did, but recalled that it was two years before he held a gun again. They taught him that there is a time to take what is sacred but to be thankful and grateful to the spirit of the animal.*

White Feather's tribe never use drugs to go into trance. They apply fasting, chanting, drumming and fatigue. The first day usually starts off with vigour and intent. On the second day exhaustion sets in and the mind starts to float in and out of what, only a few hours earlier, was reality.

We are born to undergo experience. Every day is an experience, each minute a time to explore and extend boundaries. It's hard to keep experiences at the forefront of our mind. Sadly, most are lost in day-to-day clutter. New events and contacts with people are squandered as are tastes, aromas and sounds, known but not re-lived. Experiences are not just the new but the renewal, over and over, in the delight of the present moment. Your own teacher is within you and your experiences become your library, always on hand and ready, provided you remember them. All are lessons, pieces in our jigsaw puzzle of life. They are salient processes that we must retain and draw upon.

Aching and dizzy, but with an expansion of the senses, he felt normal colours becoming iridescent. He was cold on hot days and hot on cold nights but the messages continued. Like an ox working a stone mill, round and round the pole, plodding, bare feet shuffling in the dirt, red dust plastering his sweaty frame. Grit caked the corners of his eyes. Later, in retrospect, the hardest part of the initiation was the loneliness. Although always attended by caring elders, beating the rhythm, he was on his own; no one shared the suffering or filled in the periods when his mind was not visiting the other world.

White Feather knows his ancestors. They have shown themselves to him all his life. His main guide is Smiling Courage, a mother figure who teaches him good from evil. Then there is Pine Tree who, true to his name, stands tall and straight. He encourages White Feather to be strong in storm and fury. It was Pine Tree who taught him patience, telling him that, when snow falls on the branches and weighs them down, they don't moan. They know that in time it will melt and the sun will shine again.

A necessary requirement of experience is for it to come in various forms - the so-called bad experience is a blessing that few understand. It helps to balance, and balance is required for sanity and empathy. The uncomfortable gives body to the comfortable. Experience and emotion are playmates, for emotion is the coating that we wrap around an event describing it as one to be cherished or regretted.

To his mind came another event that distressed him, a time of arrogance and superiority. *How could he take Joe's girl to play with and discard? Joe had been his friend. As children they had roamed the hills and valleys, inseparable. Losing Joe's respect was worse than losing his legs. He saw that men of knowing make mistakes, but it is men of wisdom that learn from them and that this bad time and his foolishness would make him stronger, to guide with compassion. And so, we choose our own emotions and therefore select our own worth. One person may see a lesson in an experience while another may be crushed by it. We are who we are because of our experiences, or rather the emotions we attach to them.*

White Feather travelled to realms beyond consciousness, guided in trust by spirit, seeing life's wisdom.

Many experiences are expanded beyond their importance. We forget that experiences are past events that should guide, not cripple. We must not live in our experiences as they belong to the past. Rather belong to the now.

His chants continued to the slow beat of the drum, sometimes faltering in a dry throat: *(drum) ha aay yo (drum) ha aay yo (drum) ha aay yo, (drum),* while bowed legs just supported a body depleted and exhausted.

There are those who do not learn by their experiences, who blindly grope beyond wonderful lessons, ignorant to what was being offered. To start with, we are fledglings, crawling and making mistakes, without confidence. Initially our character is formed via our genes, then our parents exert an influence; these influences are all experiences. Our environment and culture take over the moulding of the personality. Another name for personality is collective experience. As we gain in years, the distinctive trademark of our individuality is formed, more from experience and less from genes. The genes are just the skeletal framework. Our experiences put on the flesh and develop muscle to give us our identity.

On the third day, his body vomited, but as there was nothing to bring up, he shuddered violently and gagged. Acid burnt his mouth and the ferocity of the effort left him weak. Yet, so far away was his mind, it seemed to have happened to someone else.

It is what we do with our experiences that count. Do we listen to them or ignore them. Do we heed warnings? Sometimes we forget, but a remembered experience brings wisdom, allowing us to stop and say, 'I have been here before,' to change direction or continue with knowledge and confidence. With remembered experiences comes wisdom.

He knew that the initiation was over when the dreams and visions ceased and his awareness of his surroundings returned. The lessons ended as quickly as a summer storm leaves, with golden sunrays torched through parting clouds.

Bits and Pieces

Although weary, White Feather was grateful for the time shared with his ancestors. Concerned elders supported his tortured body and gently cut the thongs. He was half carried to the specially constructed wigwam to rest and reflect.

It took him weeks to recover physically but what he had learnt of experience would remain with him for the rest of his days. The time would come when he leave the white man's world, to take his place amongst his people, to guide and lead.

The Solution

I worked at JR Jones, Smith and Co for 48 years, as an accountant. For all that time, I sat in the same chair, at the same desk, in the same lime-green office. I had the same secretary working with me. We aged together doing the same work.

At first I was enthusiastic, but after several years the gloss diminished. Yet, I continued at JR Jones, Smith and Co because I was too insecure to experiment.

I caught the same bus home that I caught to work. As an accountant I knew I had done this 25 442 times!

25 442 times I came through the same gate, into my small and tidy garden and through my front door. On 23 851 of those occasions Marie was there to greet me with a kiss on the cheek. 'Did you have a nice day, dear? Let me take your coat; you must be tired. Come on in and sit down while I make you a nice cup of tea.'

One day I came home and she was not at the door to see me in. Unusual, I thought. 'Marie!' I called. There was silence in the cottage. I walked in, thinking perhaps she was on the phone. She was, but slumped over it - dead. The doctor said it was a heart attack.

The house, which in the past had been neither friendly nor unfriendly, became sombre in its silence, a place of gloom and nothingness. After my work I would sit there in a kind of stupor, while the walls seemed to close in on me.

I tried to find solace in my work, but one dismal Friday morning I was given my marching orders. New blood is what they said they needed; MBA's and bright young minds to take the firm forward.

Oh yes, they thanked me for my contribution, gave me a good retirement package and a gold watch. I don't wear watches as for some reason my body electrics play havoc with their workings. And so into the sideboard it went, as did all the personal memorabilia of Marie and my boring life. I thought, *I have a cupboard full of memories and a mind bursting with regrets.*

I was lonely and continued the same routine as if still at the office. At 10:00 I would have tea and a biscuit. At 12:00 I would read the paper and then have lunch. More tea and another biscuit followed at 3:00 and at 4:30 I would get up to go home – except I was already at home! An hour later my mind walked through the front door where it heard her say, 'Did you have a nice day, dear? Let me take your coat; you must be tired. Come on in and sit down while I make you a nice cup of tea.'

Then, some fifteen years ago, it all changed. A friend suggested that I be a Santa at the local supermarket. At first I resisted, thinking it foolish, but my friend persisted. In the end, he almost shoved me into the Santa chair just before the kids arrived.

As the first tiny tot clambered onto my lap it was like a new dawning. His little face looked up at mine, with eyes so large and round they seemed to take over his entire face. They showed his vulnerability, his trust and innocence, and in that moment a lump formed in my throat. He was only about three and half and was as frightened as I was. When I 'Ho-ho-ed' and asked him what he wanted for Christmas, he just stared at me in awe and panic.

The prompting from his smiling mother got him going as she said, 'It's OK, Ronny. Tell Santa what you would like for Christmas.'

'I, I, I wanna teddy bear,' he blurted. But, once started, he told me all sorts of things and had to be prised from my arms. I am still not sure who held on tighter, he or I.

And then he was gone and another boy sat down; his smile was wide, toothy and cheeky. Then a girl who looked like a little fairy, with blond hair fringing a face with a freckled nose. Ever since then during the festive season, there has been a stream of these beautiful and trusting young humans in my life, all blessing me with their untainted eagerness and searching for answers in my hairy face.

Oh yes, I have had my beard tugged, and fat pillow tummy punched. Many a time I have been told: 'Santa does not exist; you are a fake,' or asked: 'Where are your helpers?'

I have been asked, 'Do you really live in the North Pole? And is it very cold there?' One impish three-year old asked me, 'Did you come by taxi, because I can't see your reindeers?'

Bits and Pieces

Some of those children are now grown up and bring their own offspring. We chat and share in a mutual love of these little beings.

And when it is over for the year, I relish the thought that the following year I will again glow like the brightest star and have my time of love and joy. It will be with happiness that I pull on the Santa pants, top hat and itchy beard. Getting older as I am, I lose concentration, my voice quavers and I am not sure if my 'Ho-ho-ing' is as rich as it should be. Nevertheless I will do this work until they stop me or my clock ceases to tick.

After all of those years I have finally found myself and learnt that it is in giving that we receive.

Merry Christmas to you all!

Bits and Pieces

Turning the Tables

'Don't worry about it. It's not like you need virginity in this day and age. God, I lost mine years ago,' Janine said, as she gracefully crossed one long leg over the other.

Nicky continued to stare at the floor; a tear slid over her pale cheek and her nose ran.

Janine continued, 'Imagine, still being a virgin at your age! I remember my first time; it was in the back of ...'

'Oh, shut up!' screeched Nicky. 'Just forget it!'

Janine, shocked into silence, looked at her distraught friend. Getting a tissue from her purse, she crossed to Nicky and gently placed it in her hand. She then cradled Nicky's fair head in her arms and asked in a gentle voice, 'Did it hurt?'

Nicky continued to shudder. Her remorse was such that at first she did not answer, then she said, 'I'm sorry, Janine. I shouldn't have shouted at you but it was not how I expected it to be.'

'I know what you mean,' said Janine

'He was so ...' Nicky paused, reaching for the right words, '... animal-like.'

It was now Janine's turn to be pensive and she sighed, 'Sadly, that's what guys are like.'

Opening the gates further, Nicky blurted, 'When he was on top of me, his eyes were glazed and he just pumped to some sort of primordial beat. I could have been anyone and he wouldn't have cared! Moving faster and faster, his breath rasped in time to each revolting thrust. He was like a machine set too fast until its frantic workings exploded and he collapsed on me like a sack of potatoes. He just lay on me, panting like crazy.'

'In time you'll learn to like it,' offered Janie.

'Like I? It was horrible!' And she thought to herself: Where is the love in it? After a while said, 'You know what really pissed me off?

Bits and Pieces

Once he was dressed and about to go to his mates, he asked, "Was it good, Darlin'?"'

'What did you say to him?'

'I told him to fuck off and not come back.'

'And what did he say?'

'He laughed, threw up his arms and said, "Women! I'll never understand them!" He then left.'

Nicky blew her nose with a gurgling sound and looked at Janine in despair as Janine said," You know, Poppet, you are just too romantic for your own good."

Wiping away tears with the back of her hand, Nicky cried, 'Well, what's wrong with that? You may not care if men treat you like crap but I do!'

Janine held her tighter and, stroking Nicky's head, rocked her back and forth, as if now consoling herself. She reflected aloud. 'It's a jungle out there but I promise you one thing -- you'll learn to turn the tables and when you do, you will be the one in control.'

'I don't want to be in control. I just want to be loved.'

In the quietness that followed, Nicky's phone rang. 'Hello,' she answered and after pausing to listen, said, 'No, Joe, I'm not coming. In fact, why don't you go and screw your mates? After all, they mean so much to you.' Slowly she lowered the phone and with the first trace of a smile said to Janine, 'Is that how you turn the tables?'

Where Has Your Energy Gone?

Bailliere's Nurses' Dictionary: Adrenaline - A hormone secreted by the medulla of the adrenal gland. Has an action similar to normal stimulation of the sympatric nervous system: causing dilation of the bronchioles; raising of blood pressure by constriction of surface vessels and stimulation of cardiac output; releasing glycogen from the liver.

Yak, I feel crappy! is the thought that goes through my mind.

'Yes, you have done it again and flooded your system with adrenalin.'

Who the hell is talking in my head? I think back.

'It's me, your Higher Self. I live within you and outside you and am the link between the creator and your body's brain, a passive voice that offers intuition which, I must say, you mostly ignore. I am a silent watchdog and know every thought that your mind has and each subsequent body reaction from that thought. But it is in the management of your body's welfare that you ignore me the most. Just look at the state you are in right now!'

This is awesome. I don't believe that I am talking to you, but go on anyway.

'Thank you, I shall. Being spirit of form, I cannot be measured by scientists and so I am considered a figment of the body's imagination. Yet those same scientists make discoveries with the help of 'gut feeling'. The silly duffers don't realise that gut feeling is the same as intuition. Intuition is the main component in creativity. It is the little voice that is heard when the mind looks for an answer. I am your little voice.'

If my friends saw me talking to myself now, they would think I am nuts!

'No you're not nuts. Just chill and let me give you a lesson on your energy usage. Humans run on energy. There is the energy that drives your arms and legs. There is the energy that maintains your bodily functions. And there is mental energy; this is the strongest and takes preference over all other types of energy. Another name for mental energy is emotional energy. If energy is consumed by emotions, then there is less to use for the organs.

'Now, your body is like a battery with stored units of energy. Attached to the battery is a charger that in perfect condition keeps it topped up. But prolonged emotion uses energy in different ways. Emotions such as anger will consume large volumes of energy and can leave you feeling, excuse the pun, flat.

'If there is less energy, the organs become fatigued - which leads to disease.'

You know, you're starting to make sense.

'I can help you with your health, if you let me advise you. It is predominately your fear that does the damage. It works like this: Your perpetual fearful thoughts, even those below your subconscious, raise your adrenalin; adrenalin releases glycogen from the liver.

'Adrenalin that remains in the system for prolonged periods is destructive. It is much like taking aspirin; the system can handle small doses, but taken in large quantities has a toxic effect.

'It is not only I that will tell you emotional damage leads to physiological damage. Psychologists have said time and time again that prolonged emotions cause damage.

'The miracle of life does not demand much but there are lessons to master. Man's hardest lesson is the one based on trust – humans don't trust—*the opposite of trust is fear,* so you all live in fear, and consume energy.'

You are correct in this. I have noticed that on those days when I am anxious about something, I get tired much faster.

'Yes, it is not necessarily the number of hours you work that brings tiredness; it is the tension that is with you for those hours that matters.'

Gee, I will take more notice of you, but you don't seem to be around all that often.

'I am, but I can't shout above the babble in your mind. You have to quiet your mind so that up so my prompting can come through. Do you get that?'

Sure. You said earlier that you were my higher self. Do I have a lower self? Just joking!

Divorce

Rachael forlornly stared at the tissue while, absent-mindedly, her small hands fiddled with it. She was hurt by yet another letdown. She stared out of the window but did not see the city skyline. She was thinking that, at thirty-three, she had had all the torment anyone could take – screwed over again!

Peter knew she loved him, otherwise why would she push him away? He had come closer to her than anyone else and, as a result, Rachael had panicked and closed up. She could not handle his immersion in her very being. He was the first person to understand her and to see the hurt and pain inflicted in her past, in adolescence, and so her subconscious mind took over the conscious, the loving part of her, and killed the relationship. Ruthless in its destruction, it drew on the anger and darkness that was sown into her at the time of her various hurts. His hopes and happiness were scattered by her harshness like a wind scattering a carpet of autumn leaves.

In despair, he had no choice but to pack his things. But before he took those final steps, he had to try one last time. After all, his marriage was at stake.

'Rachael, for God's sake, we have to talk about this.'

'What's there to talk about? You seem to have made up your mind already.'

'Don't you understand? I am leaving you, not because I don't love you, but to make you realise how destructive you've become. When you argue, it is with the utmost need to win; you lie and adopt any method to belittle me. Then, when I challenge you, you deny it. Until you take responsibility for your part in our relationship, there is no relationship.'

Smoothing out a non-existent wrinkle in her trousers, she retorted, 'What about you wimping off at the first sign of problems?'

Steadying his voice, he tried another approach. 'You keep focusing on the fact that I'm leaving and not on the reasons why I am leaving. If I can't speak to you, then what's the point? Over these last months you have locked me out and, as sad as I am, you give me no choice.'

Lighting a cigarette, Peter remembered the time of their first major argument. As heated words were flowing back and forth she had said, 'I suppose you are now going hit me?'

He had been appalled. Those few words had spoken volumes about her past. His hand brushed his groomed hair in frustration as he wondered how he could reach her.

In the silence he recollected the whirlwind courtship. Like a rocket taking off, slowly at first, then accelerating upwards and going ever faster. They were married within two months - in love and inseparable. But, like a faulty rocket, the relationship suddenly reversed, screamed back towards earth and shattered into a billion pieces.

'Didn't you hear me?' she bellowed, bringing him back to the painful present. 'I said when I gave you my heart, I gave everything I have and now you're bolting and throwing it away. If you walk out that door, it will never be open for you again.'

He looked into her hazel eyes, more innocent looking because of her fair complexion,

'How can I stay when there is no communication? I talk to you but you don't hear - you don't want to hear! I want to help and support you through your problems but you won't let me.'

Peter's strong face became petulant when she was silent. He hated the silence and felt compelled to challenge her further. 'Well, aren't you going to answer me?'

She had this habit of staring at him. It was as if her mind were searching for weaknesses from which she could take advantage. The stare, he thought, was meant to intimidate him and to a degree it did. He squirmed and to deflect it, said, 'I don't know what's worse, your saying nothing or the poison you dish out when you do speak to me. For months I have tried to get you to hear me but you just push me further and further away.'

'Oh, crap! I've had to put up with your moaning ever since we met. You've become so heavy, I'm glad you're going. As soon as you're gone, I'll find someone else. There are plenty of fish in the sea and most have more to offer than you.'

She lapsed into silence, fighting an internal war between her love for this man and the need to control her environment. But her Italian culture and past indignities would not allow her to lower her defences.

He did not see what was going on in her mind, only the defiance in her eyes. Peter drifted into his own inner world and became frustrated by the futility of it all. He wanted her, but could not remain under these circumstances. It would only be later that he would realise he had fallen in love with the wrong person. He was so open and responsive, she so closed and confused.

Overwhelmed with emotion, he needed to hold her, to make it all better, but as he reduced the distance between them, she shrieked, 'Get away from me!' Aggressively pushing at him, she added, 'I don't want to touch you.' At that moment she hated him and wanted it over, so she spat, 'Go, go on, get out, I don't want you here! I am better off on my own!'

From the look on her face, he knew it was a lost cause and so, with tears blurring his vision and a heart torn in pain, he picked up his bag and let himself out.

SELFHELP

Spiritual

How We See Ourselves

Can you imagine leaving your home and life to go somewhere else to adopt a new persona? Where pretending to be different would gain you instant happiness?

You change your clothing and create a different hairstyle. In this new city you may start the process at the local hotel and act as if you were someone else, wiser or richer, maybe more confident than you really are. Later you walk, or stagger, out, feeling smug and that you have really impressed the audience.

It may be fun for a while, but like a bubble finding its way to the surface, the way you saw yourself in your old life will merge into the new. You may look and sound different, but the insecurities will be the same. The excitement of a new life and friends will diminish while your original fears will reassert themselves. Your strengths will remain strengths and your weaknesses will be just as prominent, irrespective of how many times you Clark Kent yourself into Superman. The philosophies and beliefs collected throughout your life will still assert themselves in conversations with your newly acquired friends. Your loves, hates and prejudices, of God, man and country, will cling to you as fleas cling to a dog.

The acting of a new life would, like yesterday's coat of paint, fade. The way you see yourself will place you with a new set of friends but friends much the same as those left behind. You would attract the same sort of luck and circumstances that you ran from into the new life.

You are who you are because of the way you see yourself. You can't change yourself by external trimmings. You have to change from within. It can be a slow process, much the same as chipping away at raw granite, until an approximation of who you want to be remains. But unlike art, we are never completed, always a work in progress. You can't run away from what you have become, *but you can grow towards what you want to be.*

Yes, perhaps it could be fun being someone else in a new town or country, but it would be just an act. Our little selves will still cry out, 'Here I am, please see me!'

Spiritual

Does Your Life Work?
(from Pat Grayson's Know ThySelf workbook)

Meet Zelda, who is attractive but not beautiful, slim, and always laughing. On the outside she seems motivated and determined. Her friends say that she is vivacious. Zelda always has a task to do, money to make and a future to grasp. That's on the outside. The inside tells a different story. *Her life does not work* – she has little energy and her health could be better, there is no money in her bank account and her relationships with lovers and friends fluctuate from good to stormy. Yet, *It was not my fault,* is her mantra.

On the outside she tries to be positive and do the best with what she has, '… besides, what other choice do I have? *I can't help it if I am unlucky*,' she tells all.

Zelda carries hurt and anger but this tends to be buried deep down and so she is not really aware of it. Because of a life that *doesn't work*, she has self-esteem issues, but again she is not really aware of these. Her life does not work because all of her hidden demons govern it. They rule her mind with an iron grip, telling her *what to think* or *which emotion to express*. Moreover, it sabotages her life on a daily basis.

Now Zelda's friend Wendy, on the other hand, has a life that works. She is the same age as Zelda and comes from the same suburb, yet she does not have the worry lines on her face that Zelda has. Although not rich, she is financially comfortable and can afford a pleasant holiday every year. Her health is sturdy and her marriage of ten years seems to get better as time goes on. She likes her job as a manager but does not let it interfere with her home life. She is motivated and happy, which is more than can be said of Zelda. The only difference between Wendy and Zelda is that Wendy is clear on 'her issues' and has faced them. Zelda has never taken that responsibility and so she is in a constant state of disarray.

Other indicators of a life that *doesn't work*

- A person who is accident-prone. The predominant thought is, *why me?*

Trees, the guardians of the soul

Spiritual

- Things just do not get done on time; *there is always too much to do.* This person's life is in chaos, but unlike the chaos theory, there is no organising power behind the chaos. These people are always rushed off their feet and are tired as a result. Because things don't go smoothly, panic sets in and they feel that they lose control.

- Some people lunge from one catastrophe to another, three steps forward and four backwards. Lots of catastrophes are strong indicators of a life that *doesn't work.* There is always something keeping them down.

- Tomorrow it'll be better. You have heard that one, which means avoiding responsibility for today and hoping that tomorrow will be different. That is codswallop, as it is what you do today that will influence your tomorrow.

The indications of a life that *doesn't work* could go on and on, but I am sure that you now understand.

Journey of Self

It seemed that I was born into darkness, where images could just be discerned. Roots of trees as thick as a man's body lay strewn above the ground, like slumbering serpents supporting trunks of massive height and girth. Thick humus carpeted the ground, debris from the solid canopy that hid the sky far above. It was soft to walk on, damp and mildewy. The grotto of my mind was a cold and thriving place for all manner of creepy-crawly things, things that slithered in the near dark. Leaves constantly rustled as some creature scurried away from a predator, or was the predator. Things growled and hissed as fights were often heard while combatants struggled for survival.

In this cauldron of my early life, fear clutched at my gut and was a constant companion. Somehow, some way, I knew that to stay in this claustrophobic dungeon was to be vulnerable. I had endured this tomb of mind from childhood to adulthood. But a sense niggled at my mind pushing me to move and seek something better. I did not know where this sense came from, but I felt it could be trusted. So I determined to leave the relative security of the known for the unknown, and set off to find myself.

At first my progress was slow, and for a time it seemed to get even darker, which scared me more. But as I grew and developed, I learnt that to move from one mind space to another can incur darkness, as our fear takes over. I continued the journey, stumbling on, falling over life's impediments and overcoming difficulties. For this journey of self, I was alone. I had to be, as no one could share it with me. Nor did I have any idea of the direction to take – how could I? I did not know the destination and if I did, how could I know if I had made it? Never having faced myself before, it felt awkward, like wearing a coat backwards.

It was difficult cutting through the thick bush that clung to me like a thousand silent arms – arms like beggars searching, restraining and clutching, all the time demanding. The terrain was always uphill and so my arms and legs were exhausted from the pushing and pulling as I climbed higher and higher. At times I would slip and plummet to a point where I had been some time before. I would lie there feeling

Spiritual

sorry for myself, and wonder what lesson I was supposed to learn. It crossed my mind many times to give up, as the journey was too arduous. Nevertheless, I struggled on.

After a while I started to learn the ways of my inner realm and it became easier. I developed an assurance that things would keep improving and so I was able to cover more ground. The once formidable dark and dank depths of my inner self did not seem so hostile anymore. It was the same, yet different. What had changed? I had, and as if to support my evolution, I was given beams of light that radiated through the bush, showing the way. It illuminated the jungle of my mind, giving beauty and form to its interior. But there was more journeying to be done and so, onwards and upwards I clambered.

Once I came face to face with glowing eyes, menacing from a long black shape. It snarled and spat, while its breath soured my nostrils. Had this creature confronted me in the past, it would have devoured me, but I held my nerve and it crawled away.

Although it seemed to be years that I had been on this journey, I sensed that I was making progress, as the darkness gradually gave away to light. High above through the trees was blueness. I could not understand what this was, but felt it to be friendly. As I continued, somehow I knew that my direction was correct and that each step took me assuredly to a warmer place.

Suddenly, without warning, I was out of the jungle and on a stone ledge that jutted out of the valley walls. The sun shone a golden protection, nurturing and comforting and the open space was liberating.

I looked over the jungle that had previously owned me and could see the rivers that I had forded and the scrub that had cut my hands. At the time I could not see any logic or plan to it, but now it was all so obvious and perfect. From my position of elevation, the wilds were beautiful. Yet to reach this point I had been obliged to travel through those wilds and endure the experiences.

I am now much stronger, forged in the knowledge of who I am, but I also know that the journey of self is never over, as there will be new internal frontiers to conquer. But for now I revel in the joy of knowing that I have won the victory of the journey of self.

Spiritual

Money Mirror

Snug and warm in a cosy bar, with rain and a cold surf on the other side of the window, Crockie continued, '... and I really feel mankind is close to letting go of the curse of money ...'

'What would we want to do that for?' I interrupted him.

As I said this, he was about to have a sip of his beer, but put it down and offered, 'Because money is the cause of so much that is wrong and, without money, humans would be better off. It causes major problems and taints the mind of many.' And then, as if to emphasise his point, he had a long pull of his beer.

Trying to hide my mirth at the foam on his upper lip which made him look like a middle-aged woman smeared with moustache remover, I said, 'Money is a currency of another form, a reflection of our make-up, at any given time. The manner in which we create or use it and think of money reveals what we think of ourselves; that is, provided we look.'

I continued my thoughts, 'A man-made illusion is using money as a measure of our own and each other's worth. If it were not money it would be cows, pieces of glass or pumpkins. There will always be a currency for barter and therefore a measure. Not being able to earn or hang onto it shouts loudly and clearly about who you are. So the state of a person's pumpkin will tell you a lot about the compost in the mind that grows it.'

I laughed at my joke, but he blurted. 'Crap, what about greed? Are you greedy?'

'Knowing how the universe works,' I said, I would find it difficult to be greedy.'

He looked askance at me, so I continued, 'Because there is an abundance for all, there is no need to be greedy. And if you put out greed, you'll get it back in some form or other. Look at currency this way. What better method is there to learn about yourself than through your relationship with money? After all, it is only energy.'

Spiritual

I took a sip of beer and then said, 'Consider a person who is tight with money. What in their make-up instils a need to cling to it, like a toddler with a sweet blurting out, "mine"? Generous people are functional people while the greedy tend to lack something within. Those who broadcast their wealth are saying, 'Please look at me, here I am.'

On a roll, I continued, 'What about those who believe they are not valuable enough and give themselves nought?'

'Yeah, that happens,' he agreed.

The last thing that I wanted to tell him was, 'Not having any money in the bank right now may not point to a problem as the person may be on a positive path and so the bucks will, in time, catch up to their attitude.'

Pointing to my empty glass, I said, 'And by the way, it's your round.'

Painting Your Life

Our thoughts are the energy that manifest on the canvas of our lives. We are born with a clean slate but as we take control of our existence we paint it dark, paint it light, paint it grim, paint it happy.

Our thoughts are the hands that direct the brush, the eyes that give direction, the voice that shouts the way. Gleeful feelings with trust and faith will produce a vibrant and glorious picture. Gloomy thoughts direct the brush to produce the scene of a holocaust.

The wonderful thing about life is that at any time we have the ability to paint over our work, to create those palettes of happiness and forests full of joy. Stand back, look at the painting of yourself and see it for what it is. Having done so, take the time to visualise vibrant petals of love and joy. As you are your own artist, start painting now!

To cover dark with light may take a few coats, so start in one corner of your life and gradually move over your entire composition to draw in happiness, sketch wealth, mould love and sculpt health.

Spiritual

Energy Is the Thought

Energy is the thought
That covers the canvas
A sheet so clean
At the time of birth

But the passage of time
Lays on the grime
Of worry and woe
The state of flow

The brush your hand
Of your own control
To paint it dark
Or rhythm and flow

For you to repair
Or continue as before
Of light and fancy
Or a life to despair

Spiritual

The Creator Within

Sitting in the cold house late at night, he ponders his life. His marriage had been rocky for a while, but when he ran out of money she left him. He had quit a well-paying position to follow his dream.

With only one light on in the hall to give form to the interior, he sits in semi-darkness and sips a beer - a small man, with closely cropped hair and strong sharp features, his jaw wide and strong and jutting out in a defiant way, his large eyebrows giving him a serious but kind look.

For a while he had felt sorry for himself and a bit lonely, but then the determination started to surge through his mind. He knew no one could help him. This was his calling and he had to be strong. It was his driving self, and when he felt it, he knew why he was doing this— to create something that was not there before. He also knew that most don't have the fortitude – they're too scared to follow their hearts and dreams, as if pinned to one spot.

Having another pull of his beer, he acknowledges how tough it was, but he has faith in himself that he would win. After all, what else could he rely on, if not himself? Trust is what allows us to go out on a limb.

His dream and his life are not for everyone. If it were so easy, all would do it. But they don't, and after an eight-hour day working for someone else, they head home to a family and a cooked meal.

As a creator, he is one in a thousand and has the strength to see it through. All the hardships and solitude will have been worth it, because he is a builder, a creator, a dreamer -- and so he builds and creates his dreams.

He has learnt that there is no greater satisfaction than to achieve, and to do so because he trusts and backs himself.

It has been the same since the sun first appeared over the horizon. Man painted and wrote. They were laughed at, but their pictures and words are still with us today. Men thought thoughts that were not in line with the ideologies of the time and were imprisoned or butchered. Yet their thoughts are also with us today to remind us

Spiritual

that alternative ideas are good. Look out of the window of your city house or office and you will see the creation of man. Everything you see is a monument to man's ingenuity.

As he finishes his beer and heads towards the kitchen to prepare a simple meal, he is focused. He doesn't care how many hardships still lie between him and his target; he will overcome them.

Later he turns on the TV and clicks on the sports channel. He sees a golfer, idolised by millions, but he also knows what the millions do not, that the golfer has had thousands of lonely hours of practice. When the golf is over, an athletics race comes on, and the winner of the 10 000 metres makes it look easy. But most do not know about all the pain, for years leading up to the race, of driving his body beyond what would be considered breaking point. If the runner or the golfer had quit, they would never have tasted the sweet success of trusting themselves.

He, like the runner and golfer, has faith that his rewards are just around the next corner and, like the writer, painter and thinker, cannot suppress that which is within him. His drive has scared many away, but attracted even more.

He remembers a conversation with some buddies about *What is creativity?* He feels very strongly that it comes from within, that it is not derived from external factors. This was a hard concept for him to get across and he believes that he failed to do so. He had explained that creativity comes from the same place that intuition does. They both come from the Source that sustains us, the Source that we are connected to, and which can therefore be called upon if one is open to it. After all, it was the Source that created all that there is and we are of the same form.

It is this belief that makes it easier for him to trust his ability and the Universe to support his efforts.

He goes to bed content with his direction, but wonders why more are not like him. All it takes is trust -- trust in your ability to win through, trust that there is a fair Universe that lets winners win and losers make their own way.

He sleeps well in the comfort that he is the painter, the thinker, the writer and the builder.

Spiritual

In Action There Is Hope

I have come across many people who seem to do nothing with their lives. They prefer to squander their time and leave potential talents untouched - precious lives wasted.

Man has achieved his station in the world through evolution. If he had not adapted and evolved, he would have disappeared from the earth thousands of years ago. Humanity is made up of individuals and each individual must also evolve in his or her own way. It is a natural urge to better ourselves and our lot in life. We do this through creation.

I believe that God is the most creative force there is and, if God created man in His own image, surely man can also create?

Of course he can. Look at the amazing architecture that shapes the horizons of our cities or beautiful art, computer systems and thousands of other inventions and creations. There are many, though, who sit on the sideline with their talent while watching the world and time go by.

Please don't think I suggest you have to go out and develop a new medicine or build a nuclear reactor. But I do think that there is a built-in need to become the best we can, with the tools given to us. With that comes fulfilment. I have not yet met a person without any abilities; all have something that they can do and do well. Perhaps yours is looking after children or writing, but whatever it is your job is to find your talent and to apply faith and enthusiasm to take it as far as it can go.

Life is about choice. We can choose action and hope or inaction and pessimism. *In action there is hope -- in endeavour freedom.*

It would seem to me that those who choose inaction are people of a negative nature. They would mutter, 'Oh, there is no point in doing that.'

The Australians have a wonderful saying: 'Life be in it,' - if we are not creating, we are not in it.

Spiritual

We grow as individuals by applying ourselves, irrespective of how often circumstances knock us down. Our universe is a curious place as it rewards those who try. Sometimes it does this in subtle ways and at other times in a more grandiose fashion. But ultimately all doers are rewarded.

I have heard those people, to whom I refer as inactive, say that they are happy. I doubt that they are happy, as their inactivity contravenes the in-built capacity to evolve. They are likely to be dissatisfied because of an underlying nagging to accomplish.

And so, how does action resolve negativity? It works because, by an action, you move towards taking your power back - power that you gave away when you gave up hope.

The Australians have another saying, which is half sung, 'Come on Aussie, come on,' and I urge you to come on, and remember that *in action there is hope*.

Spiritual

Self-worth

Johnny was fourteen and clumsy. He was always tripping over and dropping things. This made him feel worthless, especially when his family good naturedly joked about it, calling him names such as 'butter fingers' or 'dropsy drip'.

His worst time of the day was cleaning up the dishes after dinner. It made him mad when he heard his mother say in her singsong way, 'Now, Johnny, be careful; that dish came all the way from India.' He tried so hard not to drop anything but, as usual, he did. While cleaning up a thousand pieces of Mombai's finest, he thought, 'Gee, it was not my fault that I tripped over the toy on the floor.'

There were times at night when he could not sleep as the words 'butter fingers' or 'that plate was a present from my Uncle Clarence' played through his mind. He felt rotten and on occasions wanted to run away, but he never did.

Johnny loved playing soccer and one Saturday morning, while putting on his kit, he anticipated the game against the Gladiators and pretended to be David Beckham putting on his uniform.

The coach came into the change-room and interrupted Johnny's thoughts, saying, 'Bad news, guys. Steve is sick and so one of you will have to play goalkeeper. Now, let me see.' He thoughtfully put a finger against his lip as he scanned the team.

Johnnie's stomach turned as he had a premonition that he would be the one picked, and so he tried to merge with the clothes hanging from the pegs on the wall. The coach said, 'Johnny, take off your shirt and put this goalie jumper on.'

Johnny froze as the words 'butter fingers' reverberated though his mind. 'Well, come on,' he heard his coach say, 'it won't bite you.'

Johnny was numb he ran onto the pitch and shook hands with the opposition players. 'Why on this day did this happen to me?' He remembered the speech his coach had made at practice on Thursday: 'If we are to come top of the competition, then we must win this game. It's the last game of the season and the Gladiators have twenty-nine points, while we have twenty-eight. A draw is not good enough, we have to win!'

Standing in the goal, he looked at the spectators. The grounds were green with flashes of colour from the wintry clothes of the crowd and the bright uniforms of the players. As it was such an important game, the sidelines were packed. There were shouts of encouragement and people clapped and blew trumpets. The atmosphere was high voltage.

'Damn, damn, damn,' thought Johnny, 'I am so much better with my feet than with my hands. What if I let the team down because I drop the ball?'

The first half of the game was even, as both teams were tense and played with caution. The ball scooted up and down the field at quick and irregular intervals, while fans cheered and seemed to be part of the game. Many a sideline kick was made, as if to help the team. At half time, the score was nil all.

As Johnny headed to the change-room, he wondered if perhaps there was a God, because his prayer, 'God, please keep that ball away from me,' seemed to have been answered; not once did he have to catch the ball.

The intensity picked up in the second half and the opposition seemed more determined, with many forays in Johnny's half. Miraculously all shots were wide or did not reach the goal area.

With fifteen minutes to go Sam, the best player on Johnny's team, displayed brilliant footwork by dribbling past three defenders and powering the ball into the back of the opposition's net. The crowd erupted as one, as if the ground had risen, earthquake-like, from underneath them. Spectators jumped up and down in either glee or frustration.

Johnny jumped with them, until he remembered his position in the goal and excitement turned to dread. And so a new round of pleading started, 'God, please ...'

A few minutes later the voice of the opposing coach boomed out in a slow way, 'Come-on-Gladiators, you only have ten minutes.' This seemed to galvanise them, as if they were real gladiators and their lives depended on that one goal. Their attacks became relentless, as wave after wave saw the ball ping-ponging around Johnny's penalty box. The atmosphere was so intense that Johnny's adrenalin rose and threatened to burst out of his body. He forgot about broken cups and smashed plates; only one image occupied his mind, and that was himself and the ball -- a ball that was not going to cross his goal line.

The first time he stopped it, it was with a diving save to the right where, with his body horizontal and an arm outstretched, he just managed to finger the ball wide of the post. The crowd erupted again. Two minutes later, he tipped a thunderbolt of a shot over the bar. And soon after that, a Gladiator forward broke through and at almost point blank range, let rip with a shot that nearly took Johnny's hands off, but he held on.

He heard someone shout with urgency, 'nearly there boys, only a minute to go!' And then it happened -- the opposition winger fell over in the penalty box.

Whether it was a trip or a stumble, the penalty was given.

Johnny was stunned. He knew the entire season was to come down to one kick, a kick that he had to save. Although it was a cold day, he was sweating profusely. His heart thumped so hard, he wondered if it would smash the cage of his chest.

It seemed to take hours for the referee to place the ball on the white spot, only eleven short steps from his goal. Johnny was determined and crouched down in readiness, but just as the kicker ran to the ball, the words, 'butter fingers' flashed across his mind. And then everything happened in slow motion.

Within seconds Johnny's team-mates were all over him. Some were slapping him on the back and others were shouting, 'Johnny, you're the best!'

He realised that he still had the ball clutched tightly to his chest after his spectacular save. The coach ran over and shouted, 'Johnny, Johnny, Johnny that was the best catch I've ever seen! I knew I could trust you as goalie!'

Even some of the opposition players came over and grudgingly muttered, 'Well done, Goalie. If it weren't for you, we would have won the competition.' That night Johnny slept in his goalie shirt.

Spiritual

Years later, Johnny had a small paunch and watched his own son play soccer. He could not help the smile that came to his face when he recollected that, not once since that day had he broken a glass, a cup or any crockery at all. It still amazed him, just how brittle our self-worth can be and how we let a lack of it damage us as a result of our thought processes.

Johnny has become wealthy as a motivational speaker, teaching people about *self-worth*.

Time and People

Life slips through our fingers – a valuable and finite gold dust. Each precious grain glitters as it disappears forever, irretrievable. Yet we don't see its value and take it for granted.

Each life, like many days, starts in a burst of sunlight and fades away into nothingness at night, to recur a thousand times, all to be cherished. So too are the people who fill our lives, shining stars who have come and gone, all beautiful and a cascade of brilliance in their own time.

Take Jack, a mammoth in his day, but look at him now: plastic hips, grey dome. Only the light in his eyes remains – sadly, that will soon be extinguished.

My Uncle John, a war hero with a winner's smile, is one of the gentlest people I have known. In pain and discomfort from rampant cancer, the smile and hero's courage cling to him as he asks me about my life, while his is rotting away.

And Denny, an Angel on Earth, has helped me along the way, always with a smile.

Then there is my mother, whose strength and wisdom flow in my blood. A person of immense generosity, which will continue until she departs, no matter how blind or bent she becomes.

These four, and hundreds of others who have touched my soul, are not exceptions. All people are good; some just do bad things, as we all do on occasion. The beauty of people is what makes life worthwhile. Coming and going, like the pistons of a car, some coming up while others go down in a never-ending cycle of movement. They are like the rainstorm, now quenching the earth, soon to be gone.

To be here, even in a harsh life, is a blessing. Beware of the impermanence. Even as you read this, the grains are slipping away – you are always nearing the finish line, a finish line that, when crossed, offers no photos or medals.

Will your life have been worthwhile?

Spiritual

In Days of Old *(from Pat Grayson's Know ThySelf workbook)*

In days of old, when Knights were bold, there lived a knight in not too shiny armour. He went by the name of Alphonse.

Alphonse, a poor Knight, could not afford servants to clean his armor. He was so poor that he used to sleep in the woods. It rained a lot, which beat down with a drumming sound on his metal suit.

One bright summer day, while birds were singing, Alphonse emerged from the forest to forage for scraps in the palace garbage bins. Not watching where he was going, he bumped into a damsel.

'Wach whare y goen, y big oaf,' she screeched. Alphonse was thunderstruck -- it was love at first sight. Other than a pea-sized wart, massive beaked nose, hair like a sucked mango pip and pointy little chin, he thought her lovely. Her name was Fracila and she was a chambermaid of the Royal Guard. This was considered a lowly position, but there were perks!

A courtship followed that was to lead to marriage. It did not matter to her that he was a bit rusty; she had managed to secure her very own Knight. He did not mind her castigating him for all kinds of reasons. However, before the wedding day arrived, Fracila suggested that he go off on an adventure, not only to prove himself, but mostly in search of a fortune they could live on. 'But I won't be able fight in rusty armour,' Alphonse squeaked.

Considering the problem, she said, 'I done a vaver fo the blacksmif, I'll git im to elp. Eel getcha clean.' What sort of favour? Alphonse wondered.

She left and by and by arrived back with a sooty-skinned man, dragging a bag of tools. Introducing them, she said, 'Blacky, this is me hubby to be Alphonse; Alphonse, Blacky.'

Blacky got right to work, polishing, scraping, scrubbing and painting and after a day and a half, our Knight in shinier but still battered armour and with a borrowed donkey was ready to set off for those

Trees, the guardians of the soul

Spiritual

distant shores to seek his fortune. Avoiding the wart, he kissed Fracila and rode off into the wild-blue yonder.

Here we pause in our metaphor of life and its lessons.

- *We started the story with Alphonse emerging from the forest rather worse for wear. Clearly his life did not work.*
- *An event, a catalyst, forced him to improve himself or stay stuck where he was. Being an intrepid Knight, he took on the challenge*
- *The cleaning of his armour is a metaphor for the cleaning up of his act.*
- *Riding off was where he set out to find himself.*
- *The fortune was the reward for the finding of self.*
- *Now, we will not go into all his trials and tribulations (lessons in life) in his search; suffice to say, there were many.*
- *We pick up the story some eight years later, when ...*

Alphonse returned, resplendent in brand new armour that would make any knight of the Round Table proud. He rode regally upon a mount of such breeding and grace that he would become the talk of the land. Following Alphonse was an entourage of some fifty people. Clearly Alphonse had found his fortune.

Back to the metaphors.

Many of us have this image that tomorrow we will find ourselves. That some time in the future we will be happy and all will be well. In the story, this is what Alphonse accomplishes as he returns a hero. But, unless we do something today to improve our tomorrow, tomorrow will be just like today. Remember, this is a fairy tale and unless we solve our issues our armour will remain dull and tainted.

To continue ...

Fracila was beside herself with joy and the anticipation of wealth. She batted her eye-lashes at Alphonse as he dismounted. He seemed taller and stood with an eminence, full of confidence.

Avoiding the wart, he kissed her on the face and said, 'Fracila, we must talk ...'

Spiritual

In finding himself, Alphonse realised that he had grown beyond Fracila. He learnt that he did not need her to make him happy and that he was in charge of his own destiny. Besides, there always has to be a twist in the tale, doesn't there?

Let see how it all ends up ...

And so it came to pass that the King issued a decree awarding Alphonse a parcel of land. He also gave him a stipend for his service to the crown.

Fracila continued her position as a Chambermaid where, many a time, late at night, a knock on her door could be heard at her quarters and the clunking of metal as a sword was removed from some lonely Knight.

And so they lived happily ever after.

Spiritual

The Pain of Glass

As I awoke, it was the blood that I remembered. It was from a dream that still cloaked my consciousness.

I was on my own at a travelling fair, absorbed in the moment of swirling rides, colours, laughing children and gay music, when suddenly I was approached by a scruffy man in jeans and a leather jacket. He asked if I would help him carry something heavy.

Even in the dream, I thought of my thin frame and wondered, why me? Nevertheless I followed the man. We went past merry-go-rounds, juggling clowns and food stalls, until we reached a group of people who seemed to be a gang.

He indicated a man on the ground and, as I looked, I saw that he was covered in blood. I was told that only I could 'fix' this person. I knelt down and looked more closely. His entire face was a mass of cuts and looked like a Picasso painting, with cubed glass embedded, as if he had crashed through a window. Around each fragment blood oozed, red and dark. His lips were lacerated, as if a cheese grater had been used on them. This person was in pain, but powerless to remove the glass himself; nor could anyone else. I knew it was up to me to help him. I rolled up my sleeves, braced myself and wiggled out the first splinter. He winced, but made no sound.

In most of our dreams, we are the main person or object. Dreams, when examined closely, are wonderful tools that give us information about ourselves. I realised that it was me on the ground.

The person who was led to the body was also me, as it could only be me who could pull the glass splinters out of my face.

The worst cuts were around the lips. I was given to understand that the lips represent communication and speaking out, so this was a valuable piece of information, as the man on the ground had, for most of his life, been powerless at speaking out. I also realised that the size and sharpness of each piece of glass represented the size and sharpness of each hurt.

Spiritual

Slowly and painfully I extracted each piece or, in the analogy, each hurt, until every single fragment had been removed. But it did not end there. Even though the glass had been removed and the immediate pain reduced, there were still scars. Our face is what we present to the world and the wounds were what the world saw, or rather what we thought they saw. Although I did not see it in the dream, I realised that over time the scars also had to go. They were more than flesh wounds and represented deeper emotions.

The last part of the dream showed my face at my present age, free of scars and healed.

To summarise: We do get hurt, but it is up to us to clear our injuries, as nobody else can do this for us. Yes, it can be painful, but if we do not remove them, they bite deeper.

Finally, we become stronger as a result of our wounds, but only when we take the time to understand and clear them. If we don't, we remain bleeding and hurt.

Spiritual

Awareness

Throughout the ages it has been suggested that we think positive thoughts, and, yes, that is correct. The Bible says: *As a man thinketh, so he does* (Proverbs 23-7). But how do we keep the pantry of our mind stocked with the positive? It seems that our mind has a mind of its own and stocks itself with what it wants. And that we are subservient to our own mind, slaves to our thoughts.

I have been studying this subject for many years and know that each and every one of us is the sum total of every thought and resultant emotion that we have ever had.

It is thinking that makes things so. For instance, you may find assurance in patriotism and love your flag and anthem. And when politicians invent a war, as is the case of all wars, you go off and fight on the premise that you are doing something worthwhile for 'your country'. You return minus one leg and learned that the war was man's folly.

It was thought that gave you the patriotism in the first place, it was thought that said you must go and do what is right, it was thought that made you bitter for the invalid status that now burdens your life and it is thought that governs your suspicion of politicians.

The above shows you that emotions are the result of thought. Yes, it is thought that rules our lives and makes us do or not do things.

Most at some stage or another learn this, but knowing is not necessarily growing, not in the case of thought control. Change your thoughts and you change your life is a true statement, but have you ever tried to do this? There are times when a positive thought replaces limiting thought, but it does not last long as your mind subtly slips back and carries on stocking itself as it wishes.

I would be lying to you if I told you why minds produce more limitation than upliftment, as I simply don't know. But an analogy that comes to mind is that when born our mind is like a blank CD ready to be recorded or impressed upon. As we grow up we are told

Trees, the guardians of the soul

Spiritual

a thousand negatives, such as; no you can't do that; no you can't have this. We are told about the bogyman and to fear the dark. Yes, we are told to be scared of the dark. Hell, there is no light in the womb and we weren't scared there. Many of the people we come in contact with teach us to fear things, to hold back, have limitations. All of these are recorded on our blank CD minds. A thousand times we are told, you are too big for your boots or money does not grow on trees. So ingrained are these sayings that we take them on board as limiting truths and use them ourselves. We shower them all over the place - who do we think you are? Don't bite off more than you can chew - you naughty boy or what a bad girl you are - and what about; you are born in sin!

There are a few positives that are fed into our recordings. Without these few, we are likely to go insane. But in general the impact to the mind CD is 5 or 6 times more disempowering than empowering. And so the recordings of our negativity play in the background always reinforcing things, such as; 'slow and steady' wins the race.

Most thoughts are of the same recurring theme. Like one of those old long playing records that is stuck in the same grove, playing; *I don' trust people, I don' trust people, I don' trust people, I don' trust people, I don' trust people* several hundred thousand times in your life. Or it could be – *I would be happy if I was in a relationship, I would be happy if I was in a relationship, I would be happy if I was in a relationship, I would be happy if I was in a relationship* and so on. Rubbish in, equals rubbish out and so this is what becomes real for you.

These thoughts are mostly of a subliminal nature and play in the background whilst you shower, drive and all the other activities that fill your life.

Now, let's get back to where we said that at some time in life we learn that we are our collective thoughts and emotions, and so vow that we will change them. But nothing seems to happen and life goes on as before, with the mind manufacturing its babble of limitation.

Spiritual

So how do we overcome the grip of the mind? There is only one way and that is awareness. When unaware, the mind will rule. When you are aware of what is currently playing, you can insert your own thoughts. At first this is very difficult and takes much practice. If you want to be a good cook you practice cooking. The same applies with mind control or awareness, which amounts to the same thing. It takes practice, lots of practice. Tend your mind with the love and care that you would tend your cooking. After a while the mind will responded and will fall under your conscious command, where all thoughts pass by your observation tower. It is at this point you will be able to over-record negativity with positively, limitation with empowerment. When you fertilise your mind with - uplifting and healthy thoughts - I can and will thoughts - it will happen thoughts - love, joy and happiness thoughts, will your life start to be more in line with what it was meant to be. Gone will be the fears, the worries and limitations. And you will learn what it is really like to live. All it takes is awareness.

So what is awareness? It is not a blocking out of all thought as is the case of meditation. That has another purpose, of which I will not go into here. Awareness is a consistent and persistent evaluation of what is going on in your mind that ultimately becomes a habit.

There are 2 aspects to awareness. The first is external; take in what is around you, such as the breeze gently feathering your face or the sound of birds passing overhead. Perhaps it is the traffic in the background. Feel the soles of your feet on the ground or the weight of your backside pressing the seat if sitting. By doing so you ground yourself.
The second awareness is internal. It is scanning for emotions and of course the thoughts that could be creating those emotions. Be aware of what they are and gently replace them with whispers of joy.

As said above; you are the sum total of all your thoughts and emotions. That embodiment is a result of the thoughts and emotions that have occupied your mind the longest - meaning your dominant thoughts. You are fear or joy based as result of those dominant thoughts. Yet it can change if you have the will to instil awareness. It's up to you.

Spiritual

Mind Evaluator

The department store was brimming with anticipation, as the latest innovation was on display.

Being of a curious nature, I had to be there. After shouldering in, in a none-too-gentle way through the crowd, I got to the counter, where I saw a small gingerbread like man made from green and brown plasticine. He was sitting with legs extended along the counter, but with his back straight and vertical, much the same as an 18 month child would sit. It had the strange name of 'Mind Evaluator'.

Reading the packaging, I was amazed at the claim that he grows and shrinks according to the owner's mindset. I found it interesting to note that there was no manufacturer's name or details on the box. The salesman was not able to help and said that the shipment just seemed to arrive from nowhere! Strange, I mused.

For what was only a plasticine man, I paid a small fortune, and headed home.

After breaking open the package, I sat the little man on the coffee table next to the African Violets.

Because he looked as if he had been made from plasticine, I christened him Cine.

Sitting down on the adjacent couch, I thought about the claim on the package and pondered how it would work. After a time my mind wandered. It occurred to me that, as thought is vibrational energy, it has the power to create the lives that we are living. In addition, the world and the state that it is in is a result of all of mankind's thoughts. The implication of this is that it is not God who has created the mess that the world is in, but man and his collective thought.

These radical ideas occupied my mind for some time, until my eyes fell on Cine. Flabbergasted, I realised that he had doubled in size. Whereas, at first he had been dwarfed by the African Violets, he was now much the same size. I then remembered his name, 'Mind

Spiritual

Evaluator' and wondered if it had grown as a result of my growth in understanding from the revelation. As this latest thought came to my mind, I was stunned to see Cine expand even more.

This gave me confirmation of its function as a mind evaluator. It seemed logical that we empower or disempower ourselves by our thoughts.

I then conceived an experiment, and so embarked on a fantasy that I run whenever I need cheering up. It concerns my mother in law and goes like this: I live in the hope that some time in the not too distant future, a space ship descends on our front lawn. From this emerge the ugliest aliens that the mind can conceive. In military fashion they march into my mother in law's bedroom. A short time later they return with her and all her luggage. Up the steps they drag the screaming and kicking woman. Then, with a wink from one of the aliens, the door of the space ship bangs shut and zooms into the night sky with great speed, never to return.

As I chuckle with glee, I notice that Cine has shrunk to its former size.

It seems to grow when my thoughts are empowering thoughts or contract if the thoughts are of a negative or hurtful nature. As if to confirm this, Cine expands a few millimetres.

What a fantastic monitor - imagine having the ability to know when we have healthy or unhealthy thoughts.

It dawned on me then that from now on I need to take responsibility for my thoughts, whereas before I thought any thought that I wanted, irrespective of the obvious consequences. But now that the consequences can be measured in a tangible way I must endeavour to create only responsible thoughts.

Pondering further, I then realised that a life of perpetual growth and shrinkage from a spiritual perspective was not doing me any favours. I then wondered where my ultimate growth of compassionate and empowering thoughts could take me by the time I end this life – perhaps I could become a master! And as I developed in this

Spiritual

positive direction, how big would Cine get? Would he still fit in the house?

It was then that Libby, my 3 year old daughter, toddled in. Upon seeing Cine, she squealed with joy, "plasticine!" and before I could get to the coffee table she had swooped on Cine and remoulded him into a ball.

From that moment all of Cine's powers had gone. Yet his lesson to me had been given. Perhaps all Mind Evaluators end up as plasticine!

But it does amuse me to consider just how big Cine could have become if I had been able to continue my growth with him. Hmmm, wonder if there are any more in the department store?

SPIRITUAL

Impermanence

Ever wondered what happened to that doll or train set that you nagged your parents for when you were little? "I need it" you moaned. Yet, later, the item just drifted out of your life.

And what about people, how many 'best friends' have you had dozens I'll bet. And what about the thousands of people who have come and gone? Some left a memory, but most have been forgotten, almost as if they had never been there.

Even our bodies let go of youth and vitality. What was considered good looks become old looks. Robust health gives way to incapacity. Nothing remains the same.

There are so many examples of impermanence in life. There have been loves that have come and gone - your food, here today and eaten or rotten tomorrow. You've had houses that you thought you would never leave, that have ultimately been passed to others - you start a great job, but in time its appeal wanes. And so does our life, here now, but tomorrow... well, yes, tomorrow. Time is like a storm sweeping a beach clean, all traces gone.

So what does impermanence mean to us?

It means nothing, absolutely nothing. It does, however, help to understand how to live with the knowledge that nothing remains as it is.

Imagine, for a moment, if there were permanence. Life would be so boring - the same clothes, the same car and working at the same job all your life. One reason why you may love your partner as much as you do is because of impermanence.

With permanence, there would be less value in possessions. You would be like a spoilt kid who had received too many presents on Christmas Day. But with impermanence there is a greater appreciation. Whilst things last, they are not taken for granted. Surely it is the impermanence of this season's flowers that make

Spiritual

them so stunning to look at? And is it also not the short lived life of one of those flowers that makes us appreciate its bouquet all the more?

Is there anything that is not immune to change? If there is, I can't think of it.

But why is there impermanence in all that is around us, including our flimsy life? Impermanence spotlights the one and only thing that is permanent – the Source that created us.

As you go about your day, it may help to be aware of the impermanence of everything. By doing so, your appreciation of much will heighten.

My advice is – don't take things too seriously. Remember you are part of something bigger than the impermanence of life. Slow down a bit, lower your sights. After all, what is the point of over-working for something that ultimately slips from your grasp?

Spiritual

Oneness

As a kid I remember looking up at the night sky and being awestruck by the thousands of stars. There were so many, it was impossible to count them. Like all of us, since time immemorial, I felt small. *Twinkle, twinkle little star, how I wonder what you are,* I used to think. As I grew up, the words changed to, *Twinkle, twinkle little star, how I wonder who I am.*

I was told that what I was seeing was a part of our Galaxy, which is only one of thousands of galaxies within a universe. Pretty mind boggling stuff, when one considers that we are only very small fish in a very large pond, a pond that we don't even have the ability to measure!

A universe, as explained by my Collins English Dictionary is: *all existing things considered as constituting a systematic whole*, and my Concise Oxford Dictionary: *all existing things, the whole creation (& the creator), all mankind combined into one whole.* The Latin word universus means 'all in one, whole'.
We humans have difficulty in accepting that we are only a component of something bigger, something that we don't understand. Our egos consider that we are the centre of things. Yet in a way we are, as the following will show.

A thread is made up of many strands – strands are made of fibres, millions of them. Fibres are made up of molecules and molecules are made up of atoms. String is made of many threads and many strings make up a rope.

If a fibre had some sort of cognitive process, would it be aware that it helps to create a rope? Would it understand what a rope is? Conversely, can you consider that you are an atom in the grand scheme of things?

I recently heard on the History Channel that there are more atoms in a drop of water than there are stars in the sky. Would the atom understand that it is one of billions of atoms that help to make one of the trillions of molecules to produce a drop of water that contributes

Spiritual

to form a river or ocean? Probably not. You, in your own way, are an atom.

All matter vibrates. If you were to look at something that appears to be dead or inert, like steel, and magnify it thousands of times you would see moving atoms. Who is to say that within those moving atoms there is not a life form of some sort? Surely moving atoms constitute life.

We humans are like little atoms vibrating within something much bigger than ourselves, rather like the atoms within the steel or the fibres within the thread. We are universes within universes and our bodies contain universes within universes.

There is a paradox to Oneness, inasmuch as being part of it, we are still unique. There is no other person identical to you, nor has there ever been.

But what is the point of understanding Oneness? For me, the first thing is that I derive a sense of comfort in knowing that I am connected to the oneness and that our existence is not just an accident or coincidence. More important is that by allowing myself to connect with the oneness we are part of helps to balance my mind.

To find Oneness, we must look within (duality is external) for it is only within that we find or start to comprehend Oneness. By understanding Oneness, there is a better connection to our Source. This is how I interpret Source:

There is intelligence in animal migration, as there is in cell division and all biology. There is no shortage of intelligence in nature. Where does this intelligence come from? It must come from the Universe, the Oneness.
Another way of looking at it is to say there would be no intelligence in us if there were no intelligence behind the universe.
It is the intelligence behind the universe that I refer to as God. And that is what I have a reverence for.

Spiritual

Now, those vibrating atoms must have some form of intelligence, otherwise they would not vibrate. Therefore, by extension, clearly God is in the atoms, all atoms.

If we are part of that Oneness, and if God is the intelligence that permeates all, then we must also be God because our atoms have that intelligence.

What you have read so far are only words. Words, on their own, will never give a complete understanding of what Oneness is. They are a framework to help us understand, but that is not knowing. I do, however, know aspects of what the Oneness is, as I have experienced it through my meditations and from years of metaphysical practice. To explain it is impossible, as how does one explain the inexplicable? But once you experience it, you will know it. When you find that Oneness, you will find God.

Creating God in Our Image

So many people see God as non-benevolent and uncaring. Consequently they have no faith in God.

This of course, is natural as we see God from our tiny perspective, we create Him in our image, that is, the image we have of ourselves.

What is your image of God? Is it the one that your Sunday school teacher gave you? Or is it one of distrust as a result of things that have happened to you?

I was chatting with a friend, and she said, 'Coming from a Christian background, I find it difficult not to see God as an old man figure.' This limits His magnitude to that of a human.

Your ability to love and trust God is a result of your concept of Him. But your concept of Him comes from your own frame of reference; therefore, you cannot see the grandness.

The version of God that you see is a mirror of who you are. Because we have fear, we see God through a veil of fear. Our God is one of limitation, because we have limitations.

And how do we overcome our limited view of God?

We start off by overcoming our limited view of ourselves. We move beyond fear to love, from fear to trust.

Only when you start to see the grandness of yourself, do you get an inkling of the grandness of God.

Angel Wings

As I was browsing in a gallery, the cloud in one picture reminded me of a time years ago when, in love, I was returning from Cape Town to Johannesburg. I was looking forward to getting back and seeing the lady of my thoughts. I had reached the Free State and the road in front of me was long and straight. The pastures were flat with smoky-blue hills in the background and dreary yellow-brown grass. My thoughts were interrupted by the arrival of an SMS. Before looking at the console, I knew that it was from her and my heart warmed.

The text told me to pull over to the side of the road and watch the clouds. She said that she was sending me an angel to 'secure my way'.

I sat on the warm bonnet of my car on that cold winter day and focused on the clouds. They were large, round and fluffy, and the grey and white were accentuated by large areas of blue but the strong breeze changed the formations quickly.

At first there was nothing out of the ordinary and for ten minutes I patiently watched. Then, at the top of a very large bank, a formation grew that was clearly different from the rest. It was long and tall and as I watched, a head and body formed and then wings – wings that were large enough to ensure that I could not miss this message. For some two or three minutes it stood high and proud against a bright blue background, before it melted away.

Afterwards I just stood there, totally amazed at what had transpired. How did my girlfriend do this, or know it was to happen? There were some three hundred and fifty kilometres between the two of us and she could not see the sky that I could. Or could she?

Another SMS interrupted my thoughts with the question: 'Did you see her?'

I was bought back to the present moment in the gallery, when my current friend asked, 'Well, you seem lost in the painting; what does it mean to you?'

Oh, nothing,' I replied, 'just clouds and things.'

Robbed at Gunpoint

When I set out for my evening walk yesterday, without a care in the world, I had a shock – I was set upon by two robbers. Before I knew it, I was involved in a scuffle.

It was already dark in the quiet, tree-lined streets of my Johannesburg suburb. The robbers threw me to the ground, where the thumping on the tar shattered my sense of reality.

There was a scuffle but it was mostly me, trying to squirm my way out of there. The scuffle was brief for when I saw a gun, I gave up any resistance. At the time I expected a boot to the head. The gun bought calm; now they were able to frisk me for cell phone, wallet and any other goodies they could get their hands on. To their annoyance this walker carried no such valuables, which incited them again to aggression. They shouted 'Phon, phon, money!' in a foreign accent. All they got was the crystal they ripped from my neck.

As fast as it happened, it was over in a flash, or was it? The actual time could only have been sixty to a hundred seconds but in the stunned 'present moment' of the unfolding of the event it seemed longer.

When I analyse the attack and my resultant thought processes, I know what it feels like to be a deer powerless in the path of a lion. The fight or flight was more like fright – yet, unlike the deer, I instinctively felt that I was not in any real danger. I was aware of helplessness, but that can be a good thing as there will always be times when we have no control over a situation. We must just see it through.

When it was over, they shouted, 'Run, run!' as if to intimidate me into a panic retreat. I in response walked away with dignity, without turning round to see if they were following me or raising their gun. When only about four steps away from them, I remember taking time to thank my guides and angels for protecting me. It went something like, 'Thank you, thank you, thank you,' about twenty times in quick succession. My next thought, once I was about one hundred steps

Spiritual

away was: Why did I attract this into my life? I know that I alone must take responsibility for this happening.

Further pondering led me to feel quite empowered. I think the general response from people who are attacked would be, 'Why me, why did this happen to me?'

By making this statement we become a victim or reinforce victim consciousness. As a teacher of metaphysics, I know that what we put out we get back. If you put out a victim mentality, circumstances will arise to perpetuate that belief. If I were a victim then it is likely that there would have been anger, resentment and frustration. I felt none of these feelings. A victim is powerless to ward off unfavourable circumstances. Not being a victim I attached no emotion to the event. I do not have to live my life in fear, as the victim does.

As this happened only yesterday I have not had sufficient time to process my response or gain any clarity as to what I have done or not done to create what happened. Nor do I understand the lesson the Universe thinks I need to learn. Sometimes there is no lesson for us to learn, just an experience to be had. But as I own the reason for this happening and refuse to be a victim, it is unlikely to happen again or, at least, with any regularity.

Spiritual

Christ – the Extraordinary

In 1978, in the hot sands of Egypt, a document was found. It is believed to be one of the gospels of Judas Iscariot. The contents contained various conversations with the Christ. It consisted of forty papyrus pages and after much repair work and scrutiny by scientists, it was passed over to me. The following are extracts from this amazing document.

Scroll specimen, 934 - start

Once, with apostles Peter and John, Jesus taught us about compassion towards others and said, 'It is our brothers who teach us about compassion. When young, I had collected bread from the wealthy to hand out to the poor. There was an old lady, whose clothes were so old, they were more like webs. She was bent over with hunger and sickness. I approached her and offered her bread.

'Straightening as best she could, she smiled a smile of love and said in a voice of power and compassion, "No, my friend, give it to those who need it!"

'This, my pupils, is compassion, and it is within us all if we want to use it.'

In one extract Judas wrote: It inspires me to know that as a young man Christ also had doubts, doubts that suggest he too was of human flesh.

He told me that that he had long dialogues with God and would ask, 'How can I be extraordinary when I am not? How can I be this?' God would answer, 'My son, you are extraordinary. *Take a close look at me, for I am what you are.*'

At times he would despair of what was expected of him and when chipping wood and forming joints, his mind thought that God had abandoned him. Later he understood that he was left to work it out for himself. This he did and it taught him to trust. 'God never leaves us,' he said. 'He is always within reach.'

In another discussion, I asked Jesus, 'How can you be so loving?'

Spiritual

Christ answered, 'It is within me, and of me; it is natural to want to spread love everywhere. It flows in my house, across the fence to next door and over the valley. I cannot pass a human being or animal without love being shared, as the love I carry responds to the love they carry. So, Judas, let it live in your face, your eyes, your smile and your heart.'

The Christ often spoke about dignity; our own and the dignity of others. 'Look for the true worth in people and you will find it within yourself.'

Early one morning we were sitting under an olive tree and Mary Magdalene haltingly said, 'I feel like a failure - that I have failed you.' She said this to the Christ, but with lowered eyes, as she could not look at him. The Christ said nothing and waited patiently for her to continue.

When she did, she said, 'I have been angry, as I love you so much and have not wanted to share you with anyone. I am weak and selfish.' Her eyes continued to penetrate the tuft of grass at his feet.

'Mary Magdalene, look at me. You are of the same name as my mother and sister – I have special affection for you. Do not be concerned as to past thoughts. Only concern yourself with what is now. It is a quality of man to be selfish. A quality that all must overcome if they are to know themselves - and you, Mary, will overcome it. You will do so by love and compassion as this is also natural to you. You will all learn this, but you must be willing to be one with God.'

In one discussion, Jesus spoke about his relationship with Mary Magdalene and said, 'It is better to have loved once than to have not loved. My love for God and man has not suffered from this. In fact, love from a woman has taught me much.'

Towards the end of the Christ's life I asked him, 'It would seem that Pontius Pilate the Roman Procurator will have you crucified. Does this make you angry?'

'No,' he answered, 'He is doing what his duty tells him to do.'

I became distressed and shouted, 'How can you be so forgiving?'

He smiled and answered, 'Forgiveness, there is no need for forgiveness! I have never felt a need to forgive anyone or anything.'

'Why is that?' I asked.

'When there is love in your heart, there is no sin bad enough to warrant forgiveness. When there is a need to forgive, there is separation from love. Remember, Judas, there is no need for forgiveness in Heaven.'

Peter then asked him, 'Are you fearful?' The answer came, 'It is not wrong to fear; we all have it on occasion. But don't let it weaken you. Resolve to be strong; be with a clear mind. It is when you let your mind lose direction that fear takes you.'

Late one warm afternoon, with the sun turning the sands and hills to gold, Christ was teaching. Everyone was full of joy and happiness. It was as if joy was falling off him and covering all who were nearby.

Upon seeing one person sitting on a rocky outlet by himself, wearing a glum cloak, Jesus paused and asked, 'Brother, you are sad, what ails you?'

'It saddens me,' said the man, 'that you are so great and I am nothing.'

Jesus replied, in a voice that held such love that it could have reached the most wooden of hearts, 'I see that you are sad because you do not trust that you are good, that you are strong and that you are special. You must understand that in the entire world there is no one else like you; you are unique; you are a beautiful child of God.

'You must take hold of your abilities and apply the power of your will to a task and be the best you can in that task; then you can be great.' He paused and said, 'And brother, let joy into your heart, as without it you will fail.'

The last entry of Judas's document stated: It was not his miracles that made the Christ great, it was the love that seemed to radiate from him, like rays from the sun. It shone on everyone.

Scroll specimen, 934 - end

Bodyverse (Part One)

'Brigadier, how many causalities are there?' the Commander asked.

'Millions, Sir; the enemy has killed many of our cells in Gall Bladder, which is now partially dysfunctional. Opposing troops are infiltrating via the Hepatic Ducts towards Pancreas and outwards from there. Not only are we under attack from the inside, the Epidermis is also being ravaged. Large areas of epithelial cells are dead and as the foe captures new tissue, it destroys with a scorched earth policy.'

The Brigadier waited for his superior to respond.

'How is Bodyverse taking it? Will it survive?'

'I'm not sure, Sir. It's reeling, passing in and out of consciousness; the energy is failing and biochemical function is in disarray. But worse, Sir - fatigue has set in.'

With a quivering voice the superior asked, 'Where have you deployed the army?'

'Well, Sir, we have the Haemoglobin Brigade infiltrating Bloodstream to boost the Red Cell Regiment. The enemy is using the Lymphatic and Vascular Systems to advance rapidly throughout Bodyverse. We've detected malignant opposition as far as Left Foot. At this rate of advance, it will only be a matter of weeks before they have destroyed all the main organs of Bodyverse. Protein Force is in capitulation and Bodyverse is losing weight.'

The Commander continued, 'Are we having any success with Blood Defences? Although it is early days, it takes time for the Immune Battalions to spring into action and to combat infections. It seems that we are holding our own on further advances. But with the lightning attack of this unknown adversary, much ground is already lost.'

'Sir, do I have permission to speak freely?'

'Yes, Brigadier, go ahead.'

'Sir, if we do not rally, and soon, it won't be long before Bodyverse's systems will start shutting down. Engine Heart will slow and Blood

Units carrying much needed nutrient oxygen will diminish. That means supplies required by the Enzyme Brigade will not get through and if they are hampered in their operations, infection will advance and conquer new territory. Bodyverse's temperature will initially rise and billions of cells will burn up and more organs will be slaughtered. If that happens, the mysterious energy that enlivens Bodyverse will diminish and get extinguished. Bodyverse's ambient temperature will reduce and become cold.' At this stage the Brigadier's voice trailed off but the unspoken horror of genocide was evident.

'Brigadier, your assessment is correct. Things are indeed grim.'

'Sir, our army of Joint Protective Forces has been securing Bodyverse against invasions for eons but never have we faced such a powerful foe. Sir, is this the scourge that they call cancer?'

'I'm afraid so, Brigadier. To be precise, we that work in Brain have confirmed it is called Lymphatic Cancer. Its method is to destroy the Lymphatic Units, multiplying millions of its own white cells, thereby disposing of our White Blood Cells. Once those defences are gone, Bodyverse as we know it will be in total decline and, as you said, once our Bodyverse is cold, no life can be sustained and we will all be wiped out.'

'Sir, you are more knowledgeable about these things than I, a man dedicated to the defences. I've heard tell that there are other Bodyverses out there. Is that correct?'

The Superior spoke with reverence as this was a subject close to his heart. 'Our intelligence has indicated that there are other Bodyverses out there with ecosystems similar to ours. They are collectively called Mankind and they form part of what is known as a Universe. This is much the same as we form part of the Bodyverse. We first deduced this from studying newly generated cells. There are unknown strands of DNA that are alien to us and our needs. Bodyverse is perfect; there are no coincidences and so this suggests that we have had contact with external influences. Also supporting the belief of other Bodyverses, Cell Memory gives glimpses of things beyond us and that there is more to life than just our Bodyverse, much more, in fact. Who knows, there may be Bodyverses beyond Bodyverses. It would be egotistical to assume that we are alone.'

Spiritual

As the Commander grew silent, the Brigadier asked, 'Sir, some of the Capillaries and I were having a drink in the barrack's canteen and we postulated that if something created our Bodyverse and our many cultures of Cells, Enzymes, Bacteria, Hormones, Mucus and all the others, then that creative force could have fashioned much more than us and that it is likely that we are a very small component in a wonderful scheme of things. Sir, has Mind tried to make contact with that something beyond us?'

'Yes, for some time we have reached out to the so-called Creator and some claim to have made contact. But, sadly, most don't believe.'

The Commander, after pausing in reflective thought, said, 'Sorry, Brigadier, but there is a briefing at Mind and so I have to be on my way but, before I go, I will tell you in confidence of a strategy that we are devising to eradicate the invasive force that sickens us. Some of the wiser ones suggest that if we believe in that Power you just spoke of and if we embrace it with trust, then we can win this war. We will propagate the message that, if we all align ourselves with faith, then against all odds we can win this war.'

'Sir, do you mean to say that there is power in trust and do you really suggest that this will help to destroy this cancerous fiend?'

'Yes, Brigadier, we have had evidence to suggest this. For instance, do you remember when Bodyverse broke Right Leg? Or were you too young? Well, we worked feverishly to heal bone but it was beyond our capacity. Yet it mysteriously mended. What intelligence fused bone to bone in such a perfect way? Anyway, we were stunned at how fast it healed. Cell Memory talks about something called Spirit. But I must get going.'

'How are you getting back to the top, to Mind, Sir? Isn't it dangerous out there?'

'I am to travel via Cerebral-Spinal Fluid as that path is most direct.' Putting out his hand to shake that of the Brigadier, the Commander said, 'Go well, Brigadier. Times are tough but we have to forge ahead with confidence and believe that the creative force is on our side.' And he was gone.

Spiritual

The Brigadier, although being aware of the need to get back to his regiment, for a time sat and thought over the mystical things the Commander had spoken about. Thinking of other forms of a creative force made him feel small. He wondered what the name of this force was. Then, briskly, he got up, put on his helmet thinking, 'Can't ponder the imponderable,' and went back to war.

Spiritual

Bodyverse (Part Two)

Ten days later, the Commander was heading up a senior staff meeting in Mind. In attendance were politicians and top military people.

Standing up, he said, 'We are here in a last ditch attempt to find a way to control this menace that is destroying us. Our information throughout Bodyverse has revealed a grim and worrying affair. You have all read the report and so I shall not elaborate. You have also had time to think of a strategy and so I open the floor to you.' He sat down.

The long table held no less than fifty people - yet there was a palpable silence. No one looked at the Commander or at anyone else. Most looked gloomily at the table surface, as if it held the secrets of warfare.

'Well,' the Commander said, 'Are there no suggestions?'

'Commander,' said a voice from the other end of the table. It belonged to Governor Wallace, head of Synapse Energy Systems, a young man of considerable intelligence and expertise. He stood to address the gathering. He took off his glasses to clean them, but gave the impression that this was done in an absentminded way while he composed himself for what he was about to say.

'As the report states, we have been overrun. I don't mean to be a pessimist. In fact, most of you, through the years, have considered me to be overly optimistic. But now our forces are almost beyond hope. The cancer grows stronger each day while our troops, as brave as they are, have nothing left to fight with. It is only a matter of time until every single cell, each organ, the Arterial System, Lymph and all the other systems of Bodyverse will all ...' He did not finish the sentence, but let the silence communicate the inevitable.

'There is, however, hope. Perhaps it may be just a glimmer of hope.' His voice had developed confidence and excitement. 'Some of you will scoff at the idea, and others may be willing. I shall let the Commander elaborate, but I will tell you, here and now, we have no choice but to adopt the suggestion. I am all for it.'

Spiritual

As Wallace sat down, there was buzz of discussion as all were anxious to know what was to follow.

The Commander let it run for a while and, as it did, he surveyed the audience as if to gauge its readiness.

'We have an ally, one that we have always ignored, even though it has tried to reach us many times. Within this room we have the most advanced thinkers of Bodyverse and for many years we have pondered the question as to who we are and why we are here. Yes, collectively we serve Bodyverse, but whom does Bodyverse serve? I personally have had conversations with many of you about this very subject. And, in most cases, we have agreed that there is a power that knows the logic of it all, but is beyond our comprehension.'

Not a sound could be heard. All attention was focused on the face of the Commander and the words that he was speaking. 'After the miracle of the healing of Broken Leg, a group of us, consisting of Delano from Mucus, Colonel Boddington from the Marrow Corps, Wallace and Bonny Henderson from Casualty, worked as a group. We would silence ourselves, to shut out all thoughts and noise and to try, in some way, to connect with that mysterious force.' This was said with a sweeping arm, indicating that all could see and understand.

'We learnt that our voice is a small voice, but when we went into the silent background we heard the "big voice"'.

Upon hearing this, the audience stirred and a flurry of questions rang out: 'Did it speak to you?' 'What is it like?' 'Is it friendly and will it help us?'

Waving for silence, he continued. 'Of course we did not see it, but certainly there was a presence, a benevolent presence.' He lowered his voice as he said this and there was a gentleness that suggested that the Commander had indeed experienced some mystical force.

'Gentlemen and ladies, we are convinced there is a force that created us. And that if we believe in it, it *will* come to our aid.' The Commander's voice increased in speed from an excitement that he could not, nor perhaps wanted to control. With luminous eyes he

Spiritual

exuded an enthusiasm that had never been witnessed in this sage before.

'We have called this Mysterious Force the Creator and it will come to our aid, if we acknowledge it.'

He slowed down and cautioned, 'But we must do our bit, and that is to fight with a strong mind and heart. People of Bodyverse, we can beat this scourge.'

The atmosphere in the room was transformed; where before it had been thick and lifeless, there was now a resurgence. The commander knew that he had given them hope. After all, he reasoned with himself, a life without something larger than us to believe in is a life without value. To feel as if we are a part of our Source, is to feel at home. 'Yes!' he shouted, 'With belief, and with the Creator on our side, we can't lose!'

It was Stanton, the ever hopeful head of Epidermis, who shouted, 'I knew it! There is no way that we are an accident! I have always felt that we are a part of something very profound. I say, we adopt these principles of positive thinking and belief in our Creator - after all, if it made us, then it must be willing to support us.'

'You've gotta be kidding!' shouted Pulmonary's representative Smith. 'Our heart function has all but stopped. Don't you realise that we have lost many of our best fighters? My people are exhausted beyond belief and with at least eighty trillion cancerous cells that have converged over much of Bodyverse, you say, put trust into something external to us, to lessen our own control and responsibility? Are you crazy?'

'Perhaps,' said Wallace. 'But I remember having a discussion with you in your office in Valve and it was you who said that it amazed you, how all of the parts of Bodyverse work with such an apparent ease of synchronisation. At the time you were in awe and said it was inexplicable. Well, I can't explain it, but I know that whatever the Creator is, it is there for us. Besides, what else are you offering?'

Trees, the guardians of the soul

Bodyverse *(Part Three)*

The meeting continued for many hours. A resolution of the acceptance of a Creator and of its powerful support was drafted. It spoke of the Creator and its support, but stressed the need to be of strong mind and heart. It went on to say that life within Bodyverse could flourish again if all trusted.

There was no time to waste and the message was sent via the Electrical Circuits of the Neural System. It was headed *Urgent - Communication from Mind.*

The next morning the Brigadier was down behind Stomach, in Pancreas, trying to encourage the men to continue with insulin production, when the directive arrived. Since that discussion with the Commander, he had had a sense of support, of comfort, but was not sure how to express it.

He tore open the envelope and read the contents. It took him some time to digest the full implication, but he sensed that this was the way and the only way for the survival of Bodyverse.

In shifts he explained the new understanding to all in Pancreas. At first he was worried, but realised that most of the troops had already accepted that there was a governing force. It gave them strength that this force was supportive and benevolent. But what amazed him the most was that they were galvanised with new purpose and belief. Slowly at first and then gathering momentum, insulin production increased.

The ground fighting started from Pancreas and was fierce as the cancer was well entrenched. There was slaughter on both sides and, for a time, neither side gained the upper hand. But after a week of carnage, the Pancreas forces broke through the centre of the cancerous lines and started to control the battle.

The Brigadier's next duty call was Inflammation where, after discussing the directive, the army went into battle, with sleeves rolled up, wooden clubs and a new-found security that gave them confidence. For the first time in months they started to hold ground against the determined cancer forces.

Spiritual

That success gave confidence to the Spleen Brigade where they took up the challenge and, with their colours flying, rushed the enemy with bloodcurdling screams in a do or die effort. The Small Intestine was liberated next, followed by Bladder and Duodenum. After each successive victory, gratitude towards the Creator grew.

It was several months later, in a small room inside a well-functioning Right Kidney and in a far more relaxed meeting, that the Commander said to the Brigadier, 'Over the months, one by one, each organ, each cell, each duct has been won over and, although tired, Bodyverse has started to heal. Scorched and blackened organs are returning to a healthy pink. Haemoglobin function is normal and the Energy Systems have improved. Waste materials are excreted and lucid thought have returned to Mind.' With a smile he concluded, 'Bodyverse's lights are starting to shine.'

'Yes, it is a miracle,' said the Brigadier, 'A miracle beyond bravery, one of quantum proportions. In our last meeting you said, "If we all align ourselves with faith, then against all odds we can win this war and there is power in trust." Fortunately for Bodyverse, you were right!'

In the Name of God

He came with a message of one God and of love. For this they crucified him.

Man was given free will.

On his way to the Promised Land, Moses was given the Ten Commandments for his people. In their enthusiasm to conquer the tribes of the new land, the Israelites forgot the law - thou shall not kill - and so they killed and plundered. Was this in the name of God, or man? The killing was justified because they were the Chosen People. But who chose them? It was not God, who would not select one human to dominate another.

God gave man free will, to allow him to do as he pleases.

Was the ravaging of South America by the Spanish and the exuberance with which they carried out the Inquisition done in the name of God? Was it not man's ego that needed to be gratified?

The Christians and the Muslims fought against each other for a hundred years. One was in the name of God and the other in the name of Allah. God and Allah are the same, like John in England may be called Jean in France.

Before each battle, for one hundred years, the players from both sides in this man's game prayed to God or Allah and asked Him to destroy the enemy and to allow their team to be victorious in His name. What would the Creator have thought when polled by both sides for support? He may have been grimly amused at his progeny fighting each other and calling on their Source to intercede on their behalf. If He spoke, God might have said, 'I am your God but I am also their Allah.'

I first arrived in South Africa in 1973. This was in the thick of the apartheid era. The racial issue was bought home to me while I was waiting for a train at Johannesburg Central Station. There was a display glorifying the Afrikaner nation. A part of this was the justifying of their dominion over the coloured and black people of the country. An English bible was on display and highlighted was a section of Joshua 9:15:21: *And the rulers said - Let them live; but let them be hewers of wood and drawers of water unto all the congregation.*

In their desire to rule, the white people chose to believe that the non-white people were the hewers of wood and drawers of water. Dominion in this case did not differentiate between animals and blacks. The religious precepts were expedient to their cause.

Mohamed shared his visions of one God and of love. Although the message was clear, many have been killed and maimed. The current Jihad (Holy War) is said to be in the name of Allah and is set to purge the world of infidels.

The word Islam means *submission to God* and most have submitted but the slaughter still goes on.

When is it going to stop?

The Christians say that if you don't accept Jesus Christ as your saviour, you will be committed to everlasting hell. Would God send all non-Christians, which form the bulk of the world's population, to fire and brimstone – for ever? Would He really do that? Of course man would, but in the name of God.

God gave man the power of choice. Man took it upon himself to force his understanding of God onto others. In no religious text that I know of, did God instruct man to kill or persecute any who did not believe in God.

The Buddha spoke of oneness of all and of love. Except for a few, this has been ignored.

There can't be any other way than for God to give us free will. For humanity to grow and develop we have to be in charge of our own destiny, in our own time and way. God can't and won't do it for us. A parent is unable to walk those first steps for a toddler. The child must do it on its own, as we did it on our own. As a race we are still learning to walk.

Sadly though, we use our free will to dominate, we cite God as the reason and the mechanism is religion. Throughout history there have been many wars and persecution in the name of God.

All the main religions of the world have the same core belief, of one Creator or Superior Being, which is love, so why the fighting?

Spiritual

For God's and mankind's sake, can't we let each make their own choice without intimidation or persecution? Can we not look to that one God and respect our fellow humans, the way God intended?

When you went to school, you didn't have only one teacher, you had many and so look upon the masters as teachers with different messages. Use the Buddha as the teacher who teaches you that there are many illusions in life, all of which you create yourself. Jesus taught love, The Vedic teaches the oneness of all and Mohamed taught unity.

'That's all very well,' you may say, 'but what about people who don't believe in God?' The answer is: Fine, let them retain their own beliefs and grow in their own time, unmolested. If what we live is good, it will give them direction.

All we need is religious tolerance. You don't have to stop being a Christian, a Jew, a Muslim, a Hindu or a member of any other religion, as there is good in all religions. If a religion, any religion, leads people to God, does it matter which religion it is? God doesn't care what the religion is. It's not like football, where religious groups are teams wearing a uniform. God doesn't care if it is Christian United, Muslim Athletic or the Buddhist Red Socks.

But he does want people to live in love. This can only happen when we start to become tolerant. We must have the strength to do this ourselves and then to teach our leaders.

I don't think that any one of the main religions has got it right - God and Universal Principles are beyond our comprehension. How can we understand something that we have not really seen? How can we understand something when we experience it from our limited viewpoint and not from an external vantage point?

In our ignorance we, through religion, presume to be all-knowledgeable. Man loves ritual, symbolism, ceremonies and sacred garments. We adore churches, ashrams, mosques and temples. We find security and comfort in all of these things but they are only trimmings. Enjoy them, gain security from them if you must. But don't be fooled; they are man-made to entice and summon, like moths to a light or bees to pollen. I am not against rituals and have gained comfort from them. But I will not let them seduce me or

Spiritual

convince me that another man's religion is wrong. I will enjoy the ritual but will use it to help compose myself to be receptive to God.

Most religions have sayings of love, such *as bless you, go with God, Allah be with you, in love and light, shanti,* and many more. It seems, though, that they are only meant for those of the same faith!

During my life I have been to many religious services. Some that come to mind are: Church of England, Native American, Catholic, Hindu, Buddhist, Methodist, Shamanist, Witchcraft, Masonic, Jewish, Theosophical, Revival, Spiritualist and others. In every one of them there was one common feeling and that was that God was present. I felt it and so did everyone else. The reason I believe is because all the focus is on seeking God; and they find him.

However, it is outside the ceremony where religious man exerts himself to spread, by force if necessary, God's will. The feeling of God disappears once the Minister, Rabbi or Master lambastes all codes that are not their own. Methodists denounce Born Again, Hindus rubbish New Age and so it goes on.

When is it going to stop? Yes, love your religion but insist on tolerance and seek God, not dominance.

God gave man free will and it is now time for you to use yours to look inwards to find out what God means to you, rather than confronting others who do not share the same beliefs as you do. Focus not on others but on goodwill.

Spiritual

Help from the Other Side

Are you aware that if our Angelic Helpers left us to ourselves, we would consume and ravage each other in no time?

Devoid of their silent love and guidance, Planet Earth would be a dark swirling place of anger and hate, sliding into anarchy. It is their subtle work behind the scenes that provides a bulwark against wars and genocide.

Mortals are like children who are quietly guided by their parents to become worthwhile adults. The Unseen Ones are forever softly and lovingly prodding and supporting us.

Understand this: It is up to us to show our gratitude by reaching out to them; in doing so, we become creators in our own right, teaching and healing, continuing their service here on earth, spreading their love and gentleness.

This is not a religious belief, just a plain and simple spiritual fact. By working with our unseen helpers, we can finally claim our pre-determined position at God's side. Indeed, this is not far-fetched. Like in children's stories, all can be pure and good.

Spiritual

Is Death a Rebirth?

We enter the light of Earthly existence from the darkness of a womb. We make use of a body that constantly changes throughout life, in a steady process of degradation and finally death. But is death not a birth into an unknown form?

A visitor to Earth could assume that the sun dies when night is born, and night dies when the sun is born. One leads into the other, and so it is with death.

Hindus and people from many other religions believe in reincarnation and a round of natural lives. Perhaps the following example makes sense of reincarnation.

A leaf from a tree forms from a bud, grows to full length and turns bright green. The green turns to brown, the brown leaf falls off the tree, supposedly dead. From there it disintegrates and goes into the ground as nutrition. Who says the leaf is dead when brown and on the ground? The bud, the green leaf, and also the compost are all alive at each stage. Perhaps our round of existence is the same, fading from one form to another.

The word death, if taken literally, indicates a finite thing, but I suggest that death is the wrong word for our ceasing to exist in this form. Transition is a better term, where birth is the end of one cycle and the start of the next.

The transition from being a baby starts the process of infancy. The end of infancy is the birth of the independent child; then the adolescent develops. The death of the adolescent stage is a movement into a more responsible time and, when this passes, the period of middle age sets in, then old age. After old age comes transition to something else. Each period is growth, forever evolving towards the greatness that created us.

Even within one life we have cycles of death and rebirth. The end of one relationship may allow the birth of another or, leaving one job, we may start somewhere else.

When a human dies, the body is buried or burnt and therefore of not much use to nature, but what happens to that spark? At death our

Spiritual

mind and its contents seem to be extinguished, but is that the case? Physics teaches us that energy cannot be created or destroyed, that it continues unabated in some other form.

Who knows where we may be on a universal cycle? It is like a baton continuing forward in a relay - when past athletes fade, the baton is carried forth to an ultimate destination by others. The only difference is that our spark and our memory are passed onto each successive new form. This must be so, otherwise what would be the point?

So when do we actually die? Medical people will tell us it is when the heart stops beating, but surely death is a process that starts from birth – a gradual movement, the stopping of the heart being merely the continuation of the process.

Perhaps another way of looking at death is that **death is love** or a **process of privilege**. What else can it be? It is a process of God, where he gently leads us from illusion to reality, from human to spirit, in a never-ending cycle of evolvement.

Spiritual

Bully Beef, Dried Biscuits and the Folly of War

Exploding bombs covered them in dirt and stones. Peter was functional, but only just. He guessed that the others were also scared; nevertheless, their guns were fired with great efficiency. He did not want to shoot Japs or be shot at. *We are all God's creatures, one God, the same God but with a different name.* Yet he continued carrying the twenty-five pound shells. As he picked up the next shell, another Jap bomb landed – closer this time, about a hundred feet away. Clearly the Jap gun units had plotted their position. Somewhere close by a spotter was watching them and relaying co-ordinates by radio. It would only be a matter of time before they had a direct hit and Peter's crew of six would disintegrate. But they had orders to fire until all their shells were gone. It was not just the orders that had them working like maniacs; they had men on the front and they knew that their barrage would help those men survive their rush to claim land.

It was fatigue and fear that sent Peter's mind into confusion, whilst his body automatically continued. He thought *of the folly of war – man's war, created by man's ego, of men killing other men so as to impose their will, or kill so they would not be imposed upon.*

The loud roar of another Jap shell landing brought Peter back to the moment. This one landed some thirty-five feet away. It was so close they felt the percussion. Somehow the five shillings a day did not seem worth it. In quieter times, Peter wondered *why they were involved in this foolishness that has plagued and governed man since he first picked up a stone or stick to throw. Kill or be killed seems to be the human condition. Would there be any merit or benefit in laying down his arms or a purpose to be gained by acquiescing?* He could not answer the question.

Shells flashed all over, turning the dark of night into day and back to night again, as if by a fidgeting hand on a switch. In a flash of bluish light there was a *ping* as an enemy bullet hit the metal of the gun.

Trees, the guardians of the soul

Spiritual

So not only were they under attack from long-range armament; they now had sharpshooters in on the act. He beseeched the darkness to return. The Sergeant had radioed for help in identifying where the heavy artillery was coming from so it could be neutralised – before *they* were neutralised.

Peter's arms had long since ceased complaining about tiredness as they somehow handled another shell into the insatiable jaws. There was no talking, just ghastly action. In the background their radio cracked out new ranging co-ordinates.

Even in the heat of the battle, the question returned to plague Peter's mind. *He knew that he would not let down his grim and silent comrades or his unknown Australian countrymen crawling up that far hill.*

Another *ping* followed a flash of light. This time he heard the shot, which meant that the shooter was nearer. Peter wondered w*hat was that Jap marksman thinking? Was it God, preservation, hate; or was there a calm calculation? Ping*! This time it was accompanied by a scream as Smithy went down. With a shell in Peter's arms there was nothing he could do. 'Shell!' shouted the Sergeant. 'Come on yah bastards, get the shell in! Leave him for now.'

It had started for Peter in 1940 when he was interned at Ingleburn, inland from Sydney. With the 26 Australian Field Regiment he was thrust into the life of a gunner. Peter was five foot eight, of slim build and with an ever-ready smile, which was slightly right-sided. His green eyes were bright and looked so intently at you that it seemed as if he were hearing a conversation. His short-cropped hair was blond and he was tanned from all the outside work.

The living quarters came as a shock – with only three feet of space between each bed, and the presence of twenty-four other men per hut -- there was no privacy. The showers at the camp were cold or, at best, lukewarm and only available about every fifth day. The bed was a hessian sack with straw as filler, which was rolled out on the floor of the hut. His pillow was the canvas bag that the army provided, stuffed with army issue clothes and a few other possessions -- shoe cleaner, toothbrush, paste, shaving gear and dog-eared novels.

Spiritual

When the war had broken out, Peter wanted to join the Air Force but, owing to his poor eyesight, was ineligible for the pilots' course and was told he would become a gunner. Better than infantry, he ruefully thought.

He spent three months learning the fundamentals of placing and using guns. Fat lot of good this was, as the bloody things had been built for the First World War. They were eighteen-pounders and 105 howitzers and were transported by horse! Only in action did they work with real long-range twenty-five pounders.

His crew consisted of six men, with Joe Arnott as the Bombardier. Joe was six feet three inches tall with a magnificent physique, but ugly as sin and a bit dim. However, he was good at relaying orders. Smithy joked, 'Bloody typical of the army to pick him; he's too thick to know that the extra two shillings per day for the rank won't make him rich.' But Joe was OK and they didn't mind him. As Bombardier he was second in command to the Gunner Sergeant. The Sarge was Steve Foster, who was a 'by the book man' and drove his team unmercifully - a ranting and roaring bully, compassionless beyond reason. Peter hated him.

The rest of the crew consisted of Smithy, Bucko and Jack. They were of the same rank as Peter and became his mates. They cursed together, drank together and belittled their common enemies together -- the Japs and the Sarge.

Peter remembered with glee the event that was later to be known as 'the piss-can incident'. Early one morning, just before they were to leave Ingleburn, they carried a piss-can from the latrine and quietly placed it outside the Sarge's tent. Then, while the entire camp watched, Bucko, sporting a devilish smile imitating the voice of the Captain, called, 'Sergeant Foster, out on the double!'

With real speed the Sarge flew out of the tent, only to collide with the tin. Over he and the tin went; contents and man became one. It was a furious and disgusted sergeant who scrambled up to the laughs and catcalls of several hundred men. 'That'll teach the bastard,' said a gleeful Jack. The Sergeant knew who the culprits were, but was never able to prove it. From that time on he was a bit more humane.

Spiritual

Peter had waved goodbye to his mother, father and young sister from the rail of the departing troop carrier. But it was the pretty girl in the white dress, waving a red scarf, who attracted most of his attention. She had recently become his fiancée. He etched her farewell-waving figure into his memory as the ship slowly left the side of the wharf and the sanity of Australia.

Their first stop was Port Moresby, New Guinea. After a month of additional artillery training, their orders were to proceed to Buna, on the coast, where they were to build a gun fortification as preparation against the advancing Japs. The gun base was to be made of coconut tree logs, which they were to cut down. For this they were given two blunt axes, two shovels and a pick. Coconut trees are all fibre and the blunt axes just bounced off. Sometimes the vibration would release a coconut or two, which would cause a mad scramble. After much cursing and many blisters they finally cut down enough trees.

The work was tough and the digging of the slit trenches tiring. But they knew how important their preparation was. The hauling of the gun into position was the final job. This took hours of backbreaking work. 'Struth,' moaned Joe, as sweat spotted his brow, 'I hope we don't have to move the bugger again for a while.'

Their diet of 'goldfish', which is what they called the canned herring in tomato sauce or the bully beef with dry biscuits, brought comments such as, 'How the bloody hell are we supposed to work like slaves on this muck?'

'We haven't finished yet, men!' barked the Sarge. 'We need protection from rifle fire. Fill the empty cartridge cases with the sand from the slit trenches. Stack some in front and the rest to the side of the gun.'

Once finished, there was nothing to do but wait and think. The thinking was the worst.

They were on a saddle of land between two large hills. Other gun crews occupied positions to either side. The vegetation was thick on the lower ground, but thinner on the saddle, as it had once been used for farming. They looked out over a flat expanse of valley and hills on the other side known as Roosevelt Ridge. It was at those far away slopes that they were now firing.

Spiritual

They continued the shelling; in semi-shock Smithy scrambled to his feet. The ricocheting bullet had penetrated his arm above the elbow. On weak legs he continued his work of controlling the line, range and angle of the gun sight. Smithy, a farmer, was like an ox, big and slow, with no neck to speak of. 'Fairdinkum,' Peter joked, 'it would take more than a bullet to stop the bugger.'

Smithy's grim but focused determination inspired them all and spurred them to greater effort. Peter continued with the work - bend over, pick up a shell, stagger to the gun, place it in, and step back out of the way of the ejected shell; return with another.

'Stop!' shouted the Gun Sergeant. 'Get into the trenches.' Not needing a second call, Peter nearly dropped the shell he was carrying, ran to the slit trench and jumped in. He hit the bottom and kept his head down. All of a sudden, as if by agreement, all noise stopped. Huddled into the smallest ball possible, they waited. The silence was deafening. The Gun Sergeant whispered, 'We are waiting on Command to give us fresh co-ordinates.'

It was then that they heard a loud *whoosh* heading towards them. They knew that this missile was meant for them and so they intensified their efforts to burrow further into the trench, to be swallowed up if possible. The ground erupted and rumbled like a volcano. Shrapnel flew everywhere. Jack's right shoulder disintegrated. The roar and light from the exploding shells were bewildering, while the heat of the blast scorched their exposed and vulnerable backs. It seemed to go on forever.

Peter did not know if he should be grateful for the destruction of their gun. The Jap spotter would have seen the direct hit and assumed that the gun crew would have perished. With the firelight and the crackle of the burning gun emplacement, Peter could not help thinking how lucky they were. If the break in orders had not happened at that exact time, they would all be dead. He said a silent prayer of thanks.

In the confusion they did not see or hear the Jap who had closed in on them. Nor did they hear the landing of the grenade in the trench. Although taking the brunt of the grenade, Peter felt nothing. His subconscious mind had already taken over, as it knew he was to die.

Spiritual

One minute he was alive and rejoicing in their luck and the next he was floating, in total confusion, above the scene. Down below he saw what remained of his mangled and pulped corpse. Both of his legs were gone, as was one arm. He could not understand that his body was destroyed, yet he was somehow alive. There was no pain or noise and the urgency of the moment was replaced by a disorientating stillness.

As Peter floated higher and further away from his body, it was the pretty girl in the white dress, waving the red scarf, which filled his mind.

This story is loosely based on letters my Uncle John wrote when he served in the Second World War.

Spiritual

Can I Bring My BMW with Me?

I think I understand how the soul's thread spans different lifetimes. I also understand how my thoughts and actions in this life propel me to my next life. I have learnt that there is a cosmic plan, but get confused as it is too big for my little mind to fathom.

I go with all of this and try to live my life accordingly. There are, however, some questions to ask or rather, requests that I'd like to make of my guide, and so to create the link I compose myself for meditation.

When in that state, I ask, 'Is my guide with me?'

After a time I feel a change in atmosphere and a soothing voice, either real or imagined, blesses my ear and says, 'I am already aware of what your questions are, but I will let you ask them in your own way and time and so off you go.'

After taking three deep breaths, not so much to lower my vibration but, more importantly, to calm myself, as I know what is at stake, finally I say, 'I think I have done well in my quest for spirituality, don't you?'

'You have indeed,' says the voice.

'And don't you think that I am more compassionate and loving than I was before I started my quest?'

'Undoubtedly,' is the answer.

'My question is: When I die, or rather cross over,' (I was very aware that I should use the correct terminology), 'how do I take my BMW with me? There must be a way, a loophole perhaps, based on my good behaviour?' I quickly support my question with, 'After all, if I am to travel over there, it may be faster to use the BMW and so I could do more good work in less time. In fact, I could take like-minded passengers with me. That is, provided they share petrol expenses.'

I then shut up and waited, just as I was taught to do with a customer on a sales call.

Spiritual

The voice says, 'Well that certainly is ...,' but I interrupt him with another sales point. 'Sorry, but I remembered something that is quite important. The BMW is white and is not white the colour of spirituality?'

The voice recomposes itself and says, with an edge, 'That is an interesting request indeed. If you want to bring your BMW across with you, of course you can. But I might add that in the hereafter there are no illusions as there are on earth and your car won't be real.'

This is not what I wanted to hear and so I ask, 'Illusion -- what do you mean?'

Teacher, almost as if enjoying the moment, asks in a gloating voice, 'Are you really ready for this? Shall I explain the difference between reality and illusion?'

'No, no,' I blurt, 'I don't think that I'm ready for it; it's likely to confuse me.' After a time, I say, 'Let's forget about the car for now. What about my investments? There can't be any harm, can there, you know, as security against bad times?'

'Of course you can take your wealth with you, but I am not sure that you can spend it.' With amusement the voice continues, 'Let me ask you a question. Is security not an internal matter? Do you really think you need it over here?'

Oh shit, a wise guy, surges through my mind. I am about to ask about my gold coins, when the teacher guffaws out loud, 'Yes, a wise guy, ha ha!'

Fuming, I moan, 'OK, so you know my thoughts and maybe you can fly faster or transbilocate or whatever it is that you do, big deal.' I then shut up as it continues speaking, 'What if your next life is in India and you are a beggar? Your BMW and investments would look a bit silly there, don't you think?'

'Now you have just hit on my next question. I was sort of going to ask you if I could be spared that type of life. After all, I know all that stuff and can bypass it. What do you say?'

In a serious voice the teacher admonishes, 'Your next life is determined by this and past lives. There is no choice in the matter.'

Trees, the guardians of the soul

Spiritual

At this stage I need another three deep breaths to stop my frustration from erupting through the roof. But not giving up so easily, I ask, 'What about my ...'

That is what Oneness is made of

She leisurely washed her body in anticipation of the union and knew that the apple shampoo would be sensual to his nostrils. She dressed with care and chose a delicate and subtle perfume. Likewise, he washed, as if a ritual, and considered how connected they were.

Later, together, there was no dinner, no talking, just each other and their kisses. Caressing, they knew that something very special was to happen.

It was natural, outside on a blanket, under a yellow moon that seemed to shine just for them, their clothes already discarded.

The attention they lavished on each other was returned ten fold. When he touched her, it was he who tingled. When she smiled at him, it was her heart that warmed.

With foreheads together, they looked into each others' eyes. She did not see the blue of his, but beyond, to his very soul.

When he entered her, it was like skyrockets bursting, both whimpered with the delight of it. Their movements, so in tune, could have been choreographed – a circadian rhythm of timelessness.

As their tempo continued, a deep rumble grew within them. It grew stronger, bolder, all encompassing. Explosively, like a train coursing through his body, at the same time she ruptured in ecstasy. Together they lost all feeling of consciousness as they were both transported beyond human form. In their love, they had propelled themselves to the place where their souls came from. They were one with the Universe and the Universe was one with them. It smiled and they smiled inwardly. There was no him or her, it just was.

Holding hands in wonder, they looked around and saw or felt stillness and love. In this place, there was no fear, just oneness. At the time, he knew he was not separate from God - she felt the same.

Spiritual

Instantaneously, they were back in the physical world. He collapsed on her, she held him to her body, their sweat mingling. As his breathing subsided and her spasms slowed, they looked at each other and remembered – they will always remember.

They also understood that what they had experienced could only manifest from a loving relationship, that sex without love was worthless and held no value, just a thing to feed the ego. It was from a point of need and fear and was the opposite of all of those things that they felt when they were in that place of the soul.

They may not remain with each other, for all things change, nothing stays the same. But what they shared will always be with them.

He knew that the love did not necessarily come from him. He had drawn it from the Oneness - *because that is what the Oneness is made of.*

Spiritual

For information on Graysonian Press and their range of inspirational books. www.graysonian.com pat@graysonian.com

0450260348 Australia   -   0836101113 South Africa

About the author

Pat is an Australian, an entrepreneur, a writer, a publisher and a teacher of metaphysical and human issues. He is fifty-eight.

Other works by Pat Grayson

Know ThySelf, a spiritual self-help workbook

What would you do if you knew you could not fail?

How to Write – Right!

Yogi, the tails and teachings of a suburban alpha doggy

Workshops

Pat conducts workshops and public speaking, where he addresses both individuals and groups in private or corporate settings. All his presentations are based on his writings.

Know ThySelf, a 20-session course based on the workbook

How to Write – Right!

What would you do if you knew you could not fail? Positivity workshops. These are for companies and private groups

www.ingramcontent.com/pod-product-compliance
Lightning Source LLC
Chambersburg PA
CBHW051400290426
44108CB00015B/2099